THE COLOURS OF OUR MEMORIES

THE COLOURS OF OUR MEMORIES

MICHEL PASTOUREAU

TRANSLATED BY JANET LLOYD

polity

First published in French as *Les couleurs de nos souvenirs* © Editions du Seuil, 2010.
Collection La Librairie du XXIe siècle, General Editor Maurice Olender.

This English edition © Polity Press, 2022

Polity Press
65 Bridge Street
Cambridge CB2 1UR, UK

Polity Press
350 Main Street
Malden, MA 02148, USA

ISBN-13: 978–0–7456–5571–0
ISBN-13: 978–0–7456–5572–7 (pb)

A catalogue record for this book is available from the British Library.

Typeset in 10.75 on 14 pt Janson
by Servis Filmsetting Ltd, Stockport, Cheshire
Printed and bound in Great Britain by TJ Books Limited, Padstow

The publisher has used its best endeavours to ensure that the URLs for external websites
referred to in this book are correct and active at the time of going to press. However, the
publisher has no responsibility for the websites and can make no guarantee that a site will
remain live or that the content is or will remain appropriate.

Every effort has been made to trace all copyright holders, but if any have been
inadvertently overlooked the publisher will be pleased to include any necessary credits in
any subsequent reprint or edition.

For further information on Polity, visit our website: www.politybooks.com

Cet ouvrage publié dans le cadre du programme d'aide à la publication bénéficie
du soutien du Ministère des Affaires Etrangères et du Service Culturel de l'Ambassade
de France représenté aux Etats-Unis.

This work received support from the French Ministry of Foreign Affairs and
the Cultural Services of the French Embassy in the United States through their
publishing assistance program.

For Laure and for Anne

'. . . before the very colours of our memories fade into the eternity of silence'

Gérard de Nerval (Letter to Paul Chenavaud, April 1848)

CONTENTS

ACKNOWLEDGEMENTS

This is a book of memories based on my personal history, experiences and first-hand information and reflection. But it is also the fruit of conversations, exchanges and thoughts shared with numerous relatives, friends, students and colleagues over the past decades. I would like to thank all those who have taken part in this 'game of colours' and who have lent their support to my ramblings, obsessions and 'chromatic whims', in many cases throughout almost half a century.

My particular thanks go to Emmanuelle Adam, Irène Aghion, Odile Blanc, Pierre Bureau, Perrine Canavaggio, Yvonne Cazal, Claude Coupry, Philippe Fagot, Henri Dubief (†), Michel Indergand, François Jacquesson, Philippe Junod, Laurence Klejman, Christine Lapostolle, Maurice Olender, Anne Pastoureau, Laure Pastoureau, Caroline Pichon, François Poplin, Claudia Rabel.

Colour: an *aide-mémoire*

It is not easy to define colour. Not only have definitions, over the centuries, varied from one period to another and one society to another, but even within our contemporary period colour is not apprehended in the same way across all the five continents. Every culture conceives of it and defines it in accordance with its own natural environment, its own climate, its own history, its own knowledge and its own traditions. In this domain, western bodies of knowledge do not constitute absolute truths but only particular bodies of knowledge among many others. Furthermore, they are not even unambiguous.

I regularly take part in colloquia devoted to the subject of colour that bring together researchers from a variety of fields: sociologists, physicists, linguists, painters, chemists, historians and anthropologists. Sometimes these are joined by neurologists, architects, town-planners, designers and musicians. We are delighted to meet to talk about a subject close to our hearts, but it takes only a few minutes to realize that we are not all speaking of the same thing: where colour is concerned, each specialist has his own definitions, concepts and certainties. It is not easy – sometimes almost impossible – to share these with other specialists. All the same, it seems to me that some progress has been made and that misunderstandings are fewer today than they were thirty or forty years ago. I have been taking part in such meetings for over three

decades; and I really do have the impression that chemists and physicists are increasingly taking into account the questions and enquiries of
researchers in the humanities and that, in return, historians, sociologists and linguists are improving their mediocre range of understanding
in the domain of the physical sciences. If we all continue to do so, the
sharing of views will be increasingly fruitful.

The present work, which is partly autobiographical, concerns only
the humanities. The idea for it has germinated gradually over the years
and in the course of my research into the history and symbolism of
colours. The day came when it seemed to me that it was time to share
a number of colour memories that are linked with my own history but
also with that of a number of French and European societies and with
their customs and codes over half a century. My project was not entirely
narcissistic but it was somewhat utopian. For my desire was to record
what I had seen, lived through and felt where colours were concerned
in the course of close on six decades (from the early fifties to the present
day). Furthermore, I wished at the same time to retrace that period's
history and vicissitudes, focusing on what remained permanent and
what had changed and underlining how all this affected social, ethical,
artistic and poetic matters and even the domain of dreams. I hoped to
be simultaneously a witness and a historian, supplying not only documentation, facts, observations and anecdotes but also a critique and a
commentary. It would be a difficult, almost unrealizable undertaking
but I nevertheless devoted myself to it, even though I was well aware
that one should be wary of any historian who sees himself as a witness
to his own time. For not only is he merely one witness among many
others, but he is necessarily partial, preachy, capricious, egocentric and
sometimes grumpy ('things are not what they used to be') or dishonest,
and furthermore his memory, however sharp, is not infallible.

I found proof of this a few months ago, when I reread a work which,
in a way of which I was more or less conscious, contributed to the gen-
esis of the journal devoted to colour that I am now publishing. That
work was *Je me souviens* (I remember) by Georges Perec (1936–82).
I had read it as soon as it was published, in 1978, having already seen
parts of it in earlier, relatively private publications. In the completed
book, Perec had collected together 479 sentences or paragraphs, each
of which began with the words 'I remember' and evoked a memory that

was 'quite ordinary, inessential and common if not to everyone, at least to many'. I had long been an admirer of Perec and for years I used to call to mind some of his expressions, the platitudinous nature of which delighted me. One was the following sublime statement: 'I remember that a friend of my cousin Henri would remain in his dressing-gown all day when revising for his examinations.' Another was this confession, so accurate in its very ambiguity: 'I remember how difficult it was for me to understand the meaning of the expression *sans solution de continuité* ('without any discontinuity'). Yet another was the understated and derisory declaration: 'I remember May 1968.' But there was one sentence that particularly delighted me, positioned around the middle of the book, like buried treasure, a sentence so fine and gleeful that I fancied that, for Perec, it was perhaps the most important one in the whole collection: 'I remember that General de Gaulle had a brother called André, who was red-haired and was the assistant manager of the Paris Fair.'

It would be hard to devise words more flat, more of a put-down, more delightful, yet that sentence, every word of which I remembered so precisely, never existed in Perec's collection, not in that form at any rate. What he had written was simply 'I remember that de Gaulle had a brother whose name was Pierre, who was the manager of the Paris Fair.' So I had extended and transformed Perec's text, altered the first name of de Gaulle's brother, demoted a respectable manager into an assistant manager and, to cap it all, introduced red hair where there was no reference at all to hair or to redness. For a historian, that was pretty serious. Never mind, perhaps, the changing of 'Pierre' into 'André': in the gospels, the two are brothers and it was Andrew, not Peter, who was the first to follow Christ. Besides, André is my own second name and I do no doubt tend to ascribe to it a standing that it does not always possess in society generally. And never mind the fact that I had preferred the title of assistant manager to that of 'manager'. It was more ridiculous, more laid-back, even vaguely aesthetic. For what exactly is an assistant manager if not a literary creation, inherited from Courteline or one of his successors? But why red hair? To introduce a definitely colourful note? To emphasize the burlesque nature of this character? De Gaulle's brother, an assistant manager of the Paris Fair and red-haired, to boot! Definitely farcical.

It was also an attempt to introduce colour. Many of our visual recollections have lost their definite colours; they are not even black-and-white or black-grey-and-white. Buried deep within our memories, they are colourless. But when we summon them, deliberately dredge them to the surface, we more or less consciously tidy them up, both formally and chromatically. Our memory classifies shapes, fixes lines and our imagination provides them with colours, colours that they may never have had.

Just as General de Gaulle's brother never had red hair – either in reality or according to the pen of Georges Perec, however imaginative he was – in the same way André Breton, evoked in the first chapter of this book, may never have worn the yellow waistcoat that I ascribe to him, neither in the café of the Place Blanche, nor up on the top of Montmartre, nor in the image that those who knew him have preserved. It is perhaps my faulty memory that has allowed my unreliable imagination to clothe him in this colour. André Breton, a quite exceptional figure, is indeed linked with my early childhood and my earliest colour memory. But did I dream up this enigmatic yellow waistcoat or did he really wear it?

I hope that my readers will forgive me if, in the pages that follow, my imagination has sometimes compensated for the gaps in my memory. This book about colours is based not only on fleeting impressions, personal memories and lived experiences, but also on notes taken on the spot and scholarly digressions and remarks that might be made by philosophers, sociologists and journalists. It thus comprises many fields of observation, encompassing vocabulary and other linguistic factors, fashion and clothing, the objects and practices of daily life, emblems and flags, sport, literature, painting, museums and artistic creation. Real colours and imagined colours have combined to set on stage five or six decades of recent history of both a personal and a collective nature. A historian is well aware that the past is not only what has been, but also what memory makes of it. As for imaginary representations, they are in no way opposed to reality; they are neither contrary to it nor hostile to it. Rather, they too constitute a reality – a different reality that is fertile, melancholic and in collusion with all our memories.

1

CLOTHING

IN THE BEGINNING WAS YELLOW

Is this my oldest memory? Perhaps not. But it is certainly the oldest one in colour. When my father Henri Pastoureau definitively broke off relations with André Breton, I was barely five years old. They had met in 1932 and for nearly twenty years, despite their differences in age and celebrity, they remained linked by an intellectual friendship that fluctuated but remained solid. In the post-war years, Breton would telephone our home several times a week and would quite often climb up to visit us, right at the top of the hill of Montmartre, to chat with my father about some Surrealist project or publication. From time to time he would come to dinner, bringing me coloured crayons and paper that was by no means ordinary, for it was never white, always thick and rough and cut in irregular shapes, possibly salvaged from some printer's equipment or from packaging. For a child, this unusual paper was, I must admit, somewhat disappointing, even if Breton would sometimes amuse himself by 'painting' on it, using a potato cut in half. A little ink or water-colour paint spread on to the potato made a kind of coloured pad that could be applied to the paper to create strange shapes. Breton liked to give these a form that more or less suggested a fish and he was particularly fond of using the colour green. I have preserved several of these 'potato prints' that delighted me in my early Surrealist childhood. At that time I was unaware of the fact that in many countries of the world, potatoes served as inking pads in the fabrication of false official documents.

For my mother, those dinners with Breton constituted a daunting culinary test. He was fussy about his eating and imposed a number of rules banning certain foods. Carrots, sardines and veal liver could not be served to him at table. Peas, though, were welcome – almost obligatory. As for beer, it was 'vile' (my own opinion entirely).

Although I have no more than a vague memory of all the pictures that Breton produced as I looked on, the image of his person that I have preserved remains extremely clear. There were three distinctive features to it. It was that of a man older than my father, with a huge head and sporting a yellow waistcoat. The sound of his affected voice was disturbing to a child, but it was above all his head that scared me: it seemed out of proportion to the rest of his body and was surrounded by hair that was unusually thick and long. My friend Christian, who lived opposite and whose grandmother acted as the caretaker for our block of apartments, said that he had the face of 'an Indian sorcerer'. To us, indeed, he did seem to be wearing a mask. I am surprised that Breton's biographers hardly ever mentioned that unusual head of his, the size and features of which were so striking and which conveyed an undeniable impression of nobility and authority, even as it terrified the little children of Montmartre. Perhaps it accounted for Breton's taste for masks . . .

However, what remained most strongly anchored in my visual memory was not that face so often painted and photographed, but the colour of that immutable yellow waistcoat of a matt, warm, almost sugary hue which I could, even today, pick out from a colour chart. It is unlikely that Breton ever removed his jacket at dinner-time, in my presence, for he very seldom did so. But what was it, in the early fifties, about the waistcoat that so forcefully struck the little boy that I was? What, in reality, was its fabric and colour? Leather, suede, buck-skin? Was it just a beige, felt or woollen waistcoat that my memory transformed into a honey-coloured garment? Or was it some eccentric piece of clothing such as Breton did sometimes wear and that truly was a warm, bright yellow? (His eccentricity was borne out by the fact that, on the bridge of a ship bound for America, Claude Lévi-Strauss and others had noticed him wandering about in a strange, 'sky-blue towelling raincoat'.) I shall probably never know, for the only photographs that survive from those days are all black-and-white, quite different from the ever-coloured image in my memory. What chromatic mutation has it imposed upon a no doubt very ordinary garment? And why? To preserve the memory of an extraordinary figure who, in many ways was quite alarming? Or to reflect later images more in keeping with the Breton mythology? Between ourselves and our memories other memories are interwoven, both our own and those recounted to us.

But, after all, it doesn't really matter. In my memories, André Breton will forever remain associated with a particular shade of yellow, as will, along with him, the whole Surrealist movement. For me, Surrealism will always be yellow, a fine, mysterious, luminous yellow.

TURBULENT STRIPES

At the age of about 40, I became interested in stripes, in their history and their symbolism in European societies. They were the subject of several of my seminars at the École pratique des hautes études, which produced a book that was published by Seuil in 1991 and then translated into thirty or more different languages. It was entitled *L'Étoffe du Diable. Une histoire des rayures et des tissus rayés* (*The Stuff of the Devil. A History of Stripes and Striped Fabrics*). Finding a publisher for such a work was no easy matter: to the authorities at the Seuil publishing house, the subject seemed so trivial yet at the same time possibly dangerous. Eventually the book only saw the light of day thanks to the tenacity of the historian Maurice Olender, who was the editor of the 'La librairie du XXIe siècle' series. The cautiousness of the head of this great publishing house in itself constituted historical evidence that echoed the subject of the book itself. I had tried to show that in the West, stripes had long been considered negative or even diabolical surfaces, and that striped garments had been reserved for the excluded and the outcast. Not until the eighteenth century did 'good' stripes appear, signalling freedom, youth and support for new ideas. In the following century, these 'good' stripes, which nevertheless certainly did not supplant the 'bad' ones, adorned the clothing of children, elegant women and entertainers, eventually invading seaside beaches, sports grounds and holiday resorts.

I for my part suffered a painful experience of 'bad stripes' at a very early age, when I was no more than five years old, in the Jardin de Luxembourg. Accompanied by my grandmother, I went there every Thursday afternoon. Shy, lacking confidence and agoraphobic as I was, I would venture barely 20 metres from her chair, especially as she usually seated herself not far from the central pond, a place that I considered to be particularly perilous. In truth, I was afraid of everything and everyone: the man who rented out boats and the fierce chair attendants (in those days, use of the Luxembourg chairs – which were of a yellow ochre colour – was subject to a fee); the noisy Republican Guardsmen who, without fail, on Thursdays at 6 p.m., gave a performance of the *Marseillaise* on the band-stand; and above all the park-keepers, whose dark green uniforms reminded the child that I was of that of policemen, always hostile figures.

One Thursday, in April or May, one of these park-keepers accosted me, accusing me of having walked on a prohibited lawn, on the other side of the pond, more than 50 metres from where I was. Of course, he was mistaken: I would never have dared to stray so far or to set foot on a banned lawn. I was much too cowardly and law-abiding. The fact was that he had confused me with another little boy, also dressed in a white cotton shirt with navy-blue stripes. There were probably at least fifty children in the garden, all wearing such a garment, a bastardized version of the sailor-suits of 1900. From a distance it was not easy to distinguish one from another. But the park-keeper dug his heels in, claimed he had very good eye-sight and persisted in his accusations. When my grandmother came to my defence, he pronounced the following assured and petrifying words: 'I shall put you in prison, both you and your grandmother.' I burst into tears, clung to her skirts and began to shriek. I was absolutely terrified of this red-faced man with his Gallic moustache and over-large cap. We made off, almost running, while he waved his whistle about and shouted 'Off to prison, off to prison!' My grandmother was far too well brought-up to berate him, but, as far as I remember, a number of other people did so.

In that little drama, stripes had revealed all their ambivalence or even ambiguity and had drawn attention to a number of their traditional functions, ones which, much later on, I tried, as a historian, to study in the long term: stripes are certainly young, joyful, playful, recreational and identificatory, but they can also be misleading, dangerous, humiliating and evocative of prisons. On that day, the badness of stripes had certainly prevailed over their goodness and my pretty blue-and-white striped shirt, like the ones worn by sailors, had not brought me luck. I did not want to wear it or one like it ever again. Actually, that was just as well for, later, as the age of puberty approached, I put on weight, became a plump child and the horizontal stripes of such a shirt would probably have further thickened my all too chubby youthful figure.

As for the Jardin de Luxembourg, we were forced to avoid it for the next few months and replace it by the Parc Montsouris, which was further away and duller and gloomier. My grandmother was deprived of her usual garden companions and I could no longer watch the grey and reddish donkeys circling and defecating all afternoon, around the great lawn. That accursed park-keeper!

THE NAVY-BLUE BLAZER

I do not recall wearing a jacket before the age of thirteen. That freedom came to an end in the spring of 1960 when I, along with my parents, was invited to the wedding of my mother's former pharmaceutical assistant, a young woman who had often taken care of me when I was small, providing me with a view of the world and society that was different from my mother's. It was decided that, for this occasion, I would be bought a pair of grey trousers and a navy-blue blazer. I was already wearing long trousers, but possessed no jacket or blazer. The purchase was made in the biggest menswear shop in the southern suburbs where we then lived. I can still hear the obsequious voice of the shop assistant as he ironically remarked that 'the young man is rather rotund'. What he meant was that my thighs were thick for my age. The purchase of the trousers nevertheless proceeded without any problem.

That was not the case with the blazer; and it was my fault. I would have preferred a double-breasted blazer which, I thought, had something of the look of an admiral or even a pilot, but the odious shop-assistant convinced my mother that I was too chubby for such a garment. So it was to be a single-breasted blazer; and I was not pleased about it. The trouble was not so much its shape as its colour. I had noticed that in this shop, despite it being well stocked, the single-breasted blazers for adolescents were of a navy-blue that was less navy than the double-breasted ones. Not much, to be sure, but I was already sensitive to colours and their different shades, and I vaguely felt that a navy-blue that was not very dark was not a true navy-blue. Several of my friends from more bourgeois families than mine were already wearing blazers and I knew that their blue was different from that which was proposed for me: it was darker, denser, less purplish – in a word, less 'vulgar'.

Adolescents have their own ideas about vulgarity. In many cases they would be hard put to it to explain them or to share them with adults, but there is something about vulgarity – *their* version of vulgarity – that is absolutely unacceptable. Such was the case of this 'almost navy-blue'. In my eyes, it was unwearable, hideous and would probably make me look even fatter! It was tried on, rejected, discussed, compared, tried on again. Another shop-assistant expressed his opinion, and then the head of the department did so. He was a figure of some importance and, to my great surprise, he supported my point of view. But it was all to no avail. I could not win. A dash to the door, to get a better view in the daylight, convinced my mother that this single-breasted blazer was an eminently acceptable and a perfectly classical blue and that my whims about colours were – not for the first time – totally unfounded. The shop-assistant was smirking. The head of department was less pleased, for the double-breasted blazers were more expensive than the single-breasted ones. So I had to wear this wretched garment on the day of the wedding; and I felt a shame such as I have rarely experienced. None of my friends were present, few people knew me and it was obvious that nobody noticed that the navy-blue was not quite navy. But I felt it and knew it and that tiny difference of shade deeply upset me. I imagined that all eyes were fixed on this odious and despicable blazer.

This episode had no immediate repercussions, but it was around this time, when I was about thirteen, that I became truly conscious of my chromatic hypersensitivity. Was it a handicap or a privilege? Probably both. This hypersensitivity has placed me in absurd, sometimes painful situations, but, thanks to it, I always pay attention to colours, as I do to the settings in which they are displayed and the infinite fields of observation and reflection that they procure, thereby generating much of my work as a historian.

The story of navy-blue, to which I later devoted a number of studies, is but one example among others. Without the 'blazer affair', I might never have noticed this particular colour nuance, a shade that was for a long time difficult to obtain with the use of dyes. It was seldom to be found in European clothing prior to the eighteenth century. At this point the massive importation of indigo from the New World and the (accidental) discovery of Prussian blue gradually began to introduce a new shade that became fashionable in the second half of the century. However, it was not until much later, at the end of the nineteenth century, that, in the field of dark colours, navy-blue really began to compete with black, as became increasingly noticeable after World War I, particularly in urban life. Within just a few decades, many masculine garments which, for various reasons, were black tended to become navy-blue. Uniforms, for a start. Between the late nineteenth century and the mid twentieth, according to modalities and rhythms that varied from one country to another, various uniform-wearers, one by one, abandoned black for navy-blue: sailors, rural policemen, the police generally, fire-fighters, customs-officials, postmen, some of the military, most college and boarding-school students, cubs and scouts, top sportsmen and, a few years later, even a number of clerics. To be sure, the uniforms of all those figures did not systematically switch to navy-blue; there were many exceptions. But, between 1880 and 1960, navy-blue, instead of black, became the dominant colour for all those in Europe and the United States who, for one reason or another, wore uniforms. As early as 1920, but above all after 1950, many men abandoned their traditional black suits, jackets and trousers and switched to navy-blue garments, particularly for light-weight clothing. The blazer was the most obvious sign of this revolution that was definitively to remain one of the biggest events for twentieth-century clothing and colours.

SUBVERSIVE TROUSERS

January, 1961: a cold, even glacial winter. The heavy snow that had fallen soon after the Christmas festivities did not melt and the streets and pavements were particularly slippery. I was a third-year pupil at

the Lycée Michelet in Vanves, in a mixed class, which was a rare phenomenon in such secondary schools, where girls were definitely less
numerous than boys and were only accepted in the bottom four classes.
In public establishments, mixed classes in the last two years of education were considered to be dangerous. As a general rule, the girls were
not allowed to come to school wearing trousers. Only tracksuit bottoms
were tolerated, for physical education classes. For the rest of the time
skirts or dresses were compulsory. However, one exception could be
made: on extremely cold days, trousers were allowed, so long as they
were not blue jeans, a garment that was considered to be unsuitable or
even subversive.

Despite that tolerance, on one Tuesday morning two sisters, one a
pupil in my class, the other in the second-year class, were denied access
to the school. They had arrived in trousers and, although these were
not jeans, the door-keeper watchdogs decided that their apparel was
'disgraceful' (!) and sent them packing. The next day, the affair turned
bitter, children's parents became involved, petitions began to circulate,
and so did rumours. Some of the 'big' boys in the top and second-to-
top classes imagined the trousers in question to be titillating, possibly
very tight or adorned with frills and flounces. The younger boys, for
their part, found it hard to understand why trousers could create such a
stir, especially since both the excluded girls were shy and well-behaved
and were also good pupils. Fortunately, the argument did not last and
the affair died down. The administration retreated and so did the cold
weather. It was only when my classmate returned, one week later, that
I learned the real reason for the scandal: the trousers were red.

No red in a *lycée* of the French Republic! At least, no red clothing.
That was the ministerial order of the day for the school-year of 1960–1.
To be sure, there was no textual expression of this rule, but the tacit
prohibition almost had the force of law. In point of fact, in the lower
classes of the school, I cannot remember seeing any of my school-mates
wearing red. But in the upper classes I do remember the red scarf of one
of our art-teachers, a handsome hunk of a grouch, invariably clad in
corduroy so as to look like an inspired artist. The scarf took the place of
the tie that he never wore. His son, a young fool of my own age, copied
the gear of his father, but, as far as I remember, his scarf was a totally
ordinary brown colour.

I do not think that the trousers worn by the girls who were sent home were a violent or aggressive red, such as the red favoured by that art-teacher. They were probably a dark, matt, dull red that was widely worn in those days – unless, that is, they were tapering ski-pants, in which case they may have been a brighter, more vermilion 'winter-sports' red. But what did the door-keeper and his henchmen – and, higher up, the school administration – really fear would happen if they allowed two children thus dressed to enter the school? What harm would it have done? I hardly think that anyone could have interpreted the colour of the material worn by two pupils aged 11 and 14 as an expression of Communist ideology, a particularly disquieting kind of political and militant red. Even the school administration would not have gone as far as that. Or at least that would not have been their point of view. What obsessed them were not politics, but *mores*. Any time that a general school supervisor took a child guilty of serious misbehaviour to see the school official in charge of discipline, announcing in ritual fashion that 'this pupil has committed a very serious mistake', the disciplinarian, alarmed or even horrified, would ask: 'Is it a matter of morality?' When the supervisor hastened to assure him that it was not, he would emit a sigh of relief and the misdemeanour, however serious, would be half-forgiven. In any case, in that winter of 1960–1, no-one – or hardly anyone – in our school was interested in politics, since the danger, for the government, came not from the Communists, but from the OAS [Organisation armée secrète, the terrorist organisation opposed to Algerian independence], which had nothing to do with the colour red.

So the reasons for the rejection of red in educational institutions were more likely to be found in a particular, vague and distant imaginary representation of that colour. Without anyone really being able to explain why, red, in those days – indeed, still today and always – was regarded as a dangerous and transgressive colour. More or less consciously, its everyday symbolism suggested fire and blood, violence and warfare, wrongdoing and sin. Red was too dense, too strong, too attractive, so was set apart from other colours and was hardly granted any place in daily life. For example, it was less present than it is today in the streets (where it is still uncommon). In primary and secondary schools, in note books, hand-outs and exercise books, the only function of red was to correct mistakes, to point something out or to indicate a punishment. It was an unrewarding role for a colour that, elsewhere, was often held to be the most beautiful of all.

A PARTICULAR BLUE

When I was an adolescent, in the early sixties, jeans had already become a kind of uniform – at least for the young in the social circles in which I moved: the more or less affluent middle class. But they also constituted a garment that was accompanied by a vaguely transgressive reputation and that some authorities viewed with misgivings. As we have seen, in secondary schools (*lycées*), jeans were banned, as they were in holiday camps and sports clubs. They were, above all, leisure trousers which, despite their weight and texture, were worn in times of relaxation, particularly at the seaside. In Brittany, worn with a navy-blue pullover and a white or light-blue shirt, jeans truly were becoming a uniform, for girls as well as boys.

In those days, all jeans were blue. Actually, many adults often referred to them as 'blue-jeans', although that was not common among the young, for whom the expression was more or less a pleonasm. For instance, my grandmother and her sister, who had lived in England, were incapable of speaking just of 'jeans'. They always said 'blue-jeans', with an English pronunciation, twisting their lips in an exaggerated way and in a slightly reproving tone.

All jeans were blue, but not all were the same blue. The infinite spectrum of shades in use today, encompassing variations produced by different dyeing and fading procedures (bleached, stone-used, double stone, stone-dirty, stone-destroy, rinse and so on) did not yet exist. But the palette of blues available was already quite extensive. Each brand had its own blue, which varied slightly depending on the quality of the more or less thick cotton fabric, and also on whether other textiles were interwoven or not. The eyes of adolescents were sensitive to those different nuances of blue, to which their parents seemed oblivious (although that was to change in a few years' time), just as they were to the cut of the jeans, their fabric and their labels. There were jeans and jeans, and when they bought them the young knew exactly what they wanted and what they did not want. Not that they were always asked for their opinion. 'Real' jeans, the jeans par excellence, were the famous

'Levis 501', which were created in the thirties and had evolved hardly at all since then. Only the colour had changed: it was lighter and was available in various shades of blue, more or less pale, washed out or saturated. For the adolescents of the sixties, jeans that were too dark, almost navy, were dated, 'tacky' or even 'dowdy'. Conversely, jeans that were too pale, almost sky-blue, forfeited their swagger and authenticity. The right shade was between the two, a medium blue, faded but not too much, slightly greyish, certainly not purplish blue (total horror!), not altogether uniform but not blotchy either. In my mind's eye I can still see that nuanced shade that it is hard to define but that *had to be* (terrifying expression) proudly flaunted when on holiday, and elsewhere too, in the summers of 1960–5. The cruelty of adolescents was already such that those who wore jeans of a different blue were sometimes the victims of teasing, nagging or ostracism.

Later – that is to say, toward the end of the sixties – the general colour range for jeans was considerably diversified. The monopoly of blue was undermined, as was that of rough cotton. Corduroy jeans made their appearance, either of a uniform colour or striped and in other colours too, followed by a variety of other trousers made out of heavy canvas. New dress-codes came to light, along with new exclusive fads. From the point of view of clothing, contrary to what is sometimes believed, the years preceding and following 1968 were, for the young, a period not so much of liberty but of new exclusions, many of them more strict than earlier ones.

FROM THE GARMENT TO THE MYTH

Let us stick with jeans, today the world's most ubiquitous garment. They have recovered their dominant blues, but now that the West no longer has a monopoly and that brands and sub-brands have proliferated, along with imitations and all sorts of pirated versions, the range of blues has become almost infinite: each version promotes it own particular colour, sometimes 'customized' by its owner. Some sociologists and psychologists see this as yet another expression of contemporary individualism. However, when individual behaviour patterns all develop along the same lines, is it still a matter of individualism? That is an open question. But, at this point, let us be content simply to set out a brief history of these trousers that constitute an authentic social phenomenon.

As with all objects that are powerfully symbolic, the origins of jeans remain shrouded by a certain mystery, for a number of reasons – the main one being no doubt connected with the fire which, in 1906, at the time of the great San Francisco earthquake, destroyed the archives of the Levi-Strauss company that had created those famous trousers half a century earlier. It was in the spring of 1853 that the young Levi-Strauss (whose first name, curiously, remains uncertain), a little Jewish peddler from New York, a native of Bavaria and aged 24, arrived in San Francisco where, since 1849, the gold-rush had considerably increased the population. He brought with him a large quantity of tent-canvas and canvas sheets for wagon-covers, hoping to earn a decent living from these; but sales remained poor. A pioneer explained to him that in this part of California there was less of a need for tent-canvas than there was for sturdy, functional trousers. So young Levi-Strauss decided to have trousers cut from his canvas. Success was instantaneous and the little peddler from New York became a manufacturer of ready-made clothing and a textile-producing industrialist. In partnership with his brother-in-law, he founded a company which, over the years, steadily grew. Although the company diversified its products, it was the 'over-alls' and trousers that sold best. These were not yet blue, but were of various shades ranging from blotchy white to dark brown. However, although the tent-canvas was very tough, it was a fabric that was very heavy, rough and difficult to work with. Between 1860 and 1865, Levi-Strauss decided gradually to replace it with denim, a fabric imported from Europe and dyed indigo, only indigo. Thus it was that blue jeans were born.

The origin of the term 'denim' is controversial. It may be that it was originally a contraction of the French expression '*serge de Nîmes*', the name of a material made from wool and scraps of silk that had been produced in Nîmes ever since at least the seventeenth century. But, from the end of the following century onward, the same term had been used for a fabric of linen mixed with cotton, produced throughout southern Languedoc and exported to England. Furthermore, a fine woollen cloth produced along the Mediterranean coast between Provence and Roussillon bore the Occitan name *nim*; this too may have

been at the origin of the word 'denim'. But all this remains uncertain
and the regional chauvinism of authors who have written about these
matters is less than helpful to historians of clothing.

At any rate, by the early nineteenth century, in England and the
United States, denim was a strong cotton fabric, dyed indigo. It was
used mainly for the clothing of miners, labourers and black slaves.
Around 1860, it gradually replaced the jeans fabric, which Levi-Strauss
had until then been using to make his trousers and overalls. That word
'jeans' corresponds to the phonetic transcription of the Italo-English
term 'Genoese' meaning, quite simply, 'from Genoa'. The tent and
wagon-covering material used by the young Levi-Strauss did indeed
belong to a family of fabrics originally from Genoa and the surrounding region. These had been composed at first of a mixture of wool and
linen, then one of linen and cotton, and ever since the sixteenth century
they had been used in producing sails for ships, sailors' trousers and
canvas for tents, wagons and so on.

In San Francisco, as early as 1853–5, the Levi-Strauss trousers
had, through a kind of metonymy, adopted the name of the fabric
from which they were made. When, ten or so years later, the fabric
changed, the name was retained. From then on, jeans were cut from
denim, not from the Genoese fabric, but their name lived on. In 1872,
Levi-Strauss went into partnership with a tailor from Reno, Jacob W.
Davis, who had two years earlier had the idea of making trousers for
wood-cutters that had back-pockets fixed on by rivets. So, from then
on, Levi-Strauss jeans used rivets. Although the expression 'blue jeans'
did not appear commercially until 1920, from the 1870s onward Levi-
Strauss jeans were all blue, since the cotton denim was always dyed with
indigo. However, the fabric was too thick to absorb the colouring agent
through and through, so it could not be guaranteed as being 'fast-dyed'.
But it was this very colour-instability that actually ensured the fabric's
success: the colour seemed alive, evolving along with the person wearing the trousers or overalls. A few decades later, when the progress
made in dyeing with chemicals made it possible to dye every kind of
fabric indigo through and through and uniformly, firms that produced
jeans were obliged to fade or discolour their blue trousers by artificial
means in order to reproduce the original washed-out shades.

In the 1890s, the legal patent that protected the jeans of the

Levi-Strauss company lapsed. Now competing brands appeared, offering trousers made of less heavy fabrics and at lower cost. In 1926, the Lee company, created in 1908, had the idea of replacing fly buttons by zips. But it was the Blue Bell company (which later, in 1947, became Wrangler) that from 1919 onward became the Levi-Strauss jeans' major competitor. The powerful San Francisco company (whose founder had died, a millionaire, in 1902) reacted by creating the '501 Levis', made of a double cotton denim and faithfully retaining metal rivets and buttons. In 1936, in order to forestall any confusion with competing brands, a small red label bearing the firm's name was stitched along the top of the back right-hand pocket of all authentic Levi-Strauss jeans. It was the first time that a brand name was displayed so ostentatiously on the outer surface of an item of clothing.

Meanwhile, jeans had ceased to be just a work garment. They had become leisure or holiday wear, particularly for members of the wealthy American East-coast society who took their holidays on the West coast, where they liked to play at being cowboys or pioneers. In 1935, the luxury magazine *Vogue* carried its first advertisement for these 'classy' jeans. Around the same time, on university campuses, jeans were adopted by the students, in particular second-year ones, who for a time tried to ban first-year freshmen from wearing them. Jeans were becoming the clothing of the young and townsfolk alike, and, eventually, of women too.

After World War II, the fashion for jeans spread to Western Europe. Initially they could only be obtained from American stocks, but soon various companies established factories in Europe itself. Between 1950 and 1970, a whole section of the young progressively took to wearing jeans. Sociologists considered the phenomenon, which was largely encouraged (if not manipulated) by advertisements, to be an authentic social factor and regarded this androgynous garment as an emblem of protest and revolt.

However, from the eighties onward, many young Westerners began to turn away from jeans and to favour garments cut in different styles from different fabrics of more varied textures and colouring. For, despite the efforts made in the sixties and seventies to diversify the colours of jeans, blue and its various shades remained dominant (as they still are today). But while the wearing of jeans was declining in Western

Europe (in trendy circles, the ultimate aim from the eighties onward was never to be seen in them), in Communist countries – and even Muslim ones – jeans became an anti-establishment garment, indicating openness toward the West with all its liberties, fashions, codes and value-systems.

Having said that, though, if we try to set up a balance, reducing the history and symbolism of jeans to those of a libertarian or anti-establishment garment is an over-simplification, if not altogether false. The very colour of jeans rules that out: a blue garment is never subversive. Initially, jeans were the garb of male workers and only gradually did they become leisure-wear worn even by women and then by all social classes and categories. At no point, even in the most recent decades, did the young establish a monopoly over them. When one looks closely at the matter – that is, when one takes the trouble to consider, as a whole, the jeans worn in North America and Europe between the late nineteenth century and the early twentieth – one realizes that a pair of jeans is an ordinary garment, worn by ordinary people who are neither showing off nor rebellious, let alone transgressing anything at all. They simply want to wear trousers that are sturdy, sober and functional. In short, a pair of jeans is a neutral garment.

COLOUR AGAINST FLESH

I have hardly any recollections of underwear, certainly not of my own. When was it that boys of my generation took to wearing vests or underpants that were not white? I have forgotten. I may already have been attending the *lycée* when first sky-blue, then navy-blue made their appearance. But I do remember, around about the same period, what a grotesque flock we formed on the day of the school's annual medical visit: all of us clad in white.

On the other hand, I have a much clearer memory of the catalogues of feminine lingerie that my friends and I, aged 14 or 15, used to contemplate with early stirrings of desire. These were not sordid, specialized publications but simply the 'lingerie' pages of large mail-order catalogues. They contained plenty of photographs of pretty models clad in underwear, and there was no need to view them clandestinely.

The range of colours was already quite diverse. It is true that bright colours were rare and black was less frequent than it is today. But the series of pastel shades was extensive, ranging from sky-blue to pale pink or mauve and taking in fresh greens and creamy yellows, not to mention flesh-coloured tones such as 'neutral', ivory, champagne, sandy, ash-grey and a number of others. That colour range, more varied than in the previous generation but less bright and unrestrained than nowadays, is in itself very indicative. I did not spot this at the time and only realized it fifteen or so years later when, as a young researcher, I was beginning to work on the history of colours and dress-codes.

In Europe, for centuries, all clothing and fabrics in contact with the body were white or undyed for reasons at once practical (to clean them, you had to boil them, and this faded any colours), hygienic (white, the symbol of purity, never blemished anything) and also moral (bright colours were considered transgressive). Then, little by little, between the mid nineteenth century and the mid twentieth, the white of undergarments, shirts, sheets, mattresses and towels turned into colour, thanks to the introduction of either pastel shades or stripes (white in association with a colour that it 'broke up'). What was still uncommon in the 1830s was relatively unexceptional one century later: dressing in pink underwear, a light blue petticoat or a pale green blouse; drying oneself with a beige towel or sleeping on a striped mattress. Later, from the end of the 1960s onward, white and neutral colours became less omnipresent and, alongside pastel tints, brighter, clearer and more deeply saturated colours made their appearance. My generation and that of my children, little by little, violated taboos that had been unquestioned by our grandparents and great-grandparents: wearing lemon-yellow or navy-blue underclothes, sleeping between blood-red, purple or even black sheets. Black sheets! Are there really men and women who sleep in black sheets? I do not know any, but over the past twenty or so years, I have seen such sheets for sale, in shops as well as in catalogues. Do they really sell? I find it hard to believe. To sleep in black sheets: is that not to risk nocturnal visits from the Devil? . . .

But let us return to those subtly coded feminine undergarments. From the sixties onward, as the colour range became more diversified, not only in small marginal or disruptive circles but in social classes right across the board, colours did turn into veritable codes that advertisements were quick to seize upon: 'Tell me what colours you are wearing under your dress or your trousers and I will tell you who you are' (or at least what image you have of yourself or wish to convey). But those codes evolved, then rapidly lost their power, as did the fate reserved for the colour black. In contrast to white, that well-behaved and hygienic colour, black was for a while considered to be erotic, immoral, reserved for professional debauchery. But in the course of the last two decades of the twentieth century it totally lost that status and became so ordinary that it turned into the most favoured colour for women's underwear. Some women preferred black to white underwear when wearing a black skirt or blouse. Others thought that black was best suited to their skin-colour. Yet others – and many of them – reckoned that where modern synthetic fabrics were concerned, black was the dye that was least affected by frequent washing. The blackness of a pair of knickers or a bra no longer had any transgressive or even erotic dimension.

White, meanwhile, had perhaps become less innocent than in the past. It was the colour that men now most often picked when asked which was the colour that, when placed against a woman's skin, evoked a reaction of desire in them. So was purity arousing impure appetites? Actually, though, in this day and age, might it not be red, rather than black or white, that has quietly taken over the alluring, if not libertine, role in this domain? Maybe. But, nowadays, are there any colours that are still seductive or erotic, whatever the domain? Are there any colours that retain some of their mystery or symbolism and manage to elude the cunning and violence of commercialism? I think not.

NEUTRAL SHADES IN GOOD TASTE

Pierre Bourdieu's *La Distinction. Critique sociale du jugement* (*Distinction*, tr. Richard Nice, Harvard University Press, 1984), published by the Editions de Minuit, appeared in 1979. It created a great stir in intellectual and university circles and also sold well in bookshops. It had been widely reviewed in the press, and the educated public followed suit. Yet it was not an easy book to read and could be interpreted in different ways. In the first place, the word 'distinction' was ambiguous. The enquiries described in the book were based on observations made in the field and personal accounts, but also on arid statistical data. At the heart of the book were tastes, codes, patterns of behaviour, the tension between distinction and vulgarity, and the hierarchization of the social space, expressed not simply by economic capital (a Marxist idea) but also, and even more particularly, by cultural capital, here converted into 'symbolic' capital. According to Bourdieu, the dominant classes impose that domination not so much by the possession of wealth and the tools of production, but by imposing the legitimacy of their own tastes and values.

I remember having purchased the book as soon as it appeared and having discussed it at length with my circle of acquaintances, in particular my uncle and several of my female friends. Amid the assortment of examples presented, fields observed and styles of life studied, I was struck by two absences: first names and colours. As I saw it, these represented two criteria of distinction that had pervaded French society for many long decades. How was it that Bourdieu had not thought of them? All our lives, our first names classify us, often handicapping us or making us suffer throughout our existence. In college, in high school, in the labour market and in relationships of friendship and love, we are – whether we want it or not – judged by our first names. Along with one's surname and physical appearance, alas, first names are one of the foremost criteria of social distinction. Perhaps the reason why Bourdieu did not think of this was because he himself bore a first name that, in his generation, did not stand out much: it was common but not too common, and present in all social circles. *Pierre* signalled nothing by way of social origins. Bourdieu claims to have suffered greatly from his origins, but he probably never suffered on account of his first name.

So the absence of any enquiry into first names or any reflection upon them is perhaps understandable. But what about colours? How could a book that affords such attention to clothing practices and codes pass in silence over the problems of colour? Was Bourdieu not sensitive to colour? Had he never appreciated its importance? Did he, perhaps, regard it as no more than an anecdotal and insignificant 'aesthetic field'? Or was he unwilling to venture on to this shifting, almost totally elusive terrain? Like historians, sociologists are never at ease with colours: they consider them to be resistant to analysis.

Maybe Bourdieu lacked genuine informers in this domain. The subtleties of clothing where colours are concerned are primarily a bourgeois preoccupation. And those 'bourgeois' set on stage by *La*

Distinction are, for the most part, not true bourgeois. In many cases they merge with the 'ruling class', or even sometimes with upstarts. But the real bourgeoisie is to be found elsewhere. Contrary to what Bourdieu seems to believe, the 'true' bourgeoisie is not the high bourgeoisie, but the middle bourgeoisie. It is neither particularly wealthy nor fixated on power. It constructs its 'life-styles' around values that an outside eye can barely apprehend and in many cases distorts, or sometimes even invents.

I myself was fortunate enough to be born into a family of bohemian intellectuals, not rich, not poor, not even 'middling'. My parents had long since dissociated themselves from bourgeois values, which, in any case, had been those of not their parents but their grandparents. However, in my adolescent days, several of my close friends did belong to circles in which those values were still honoured. Because they were strange to me, I was both irritated and fascinated by them. Of course, my view, like Bourdieu's, was external and therefore distorting. It was different too: 'my' bourgeois were more 'old France', closer to a vague, waning, minor nobility than to opulent *nouveaux-riches* or captains of industry who were close to the seats of power. In those circles, everything was a matter of tradition. Not to behave as was customary stemmed not from anti-conformism or even immodesty; it was quite simply cretinous. In fact, anti-conformism consisted precisely in behaving in the customary fashion. And the two social classes from which it was absolutely necessary to distinguish oneself had no connections with the rural world (on the contrary, for peasants were 'respectable' people); no, they belonged to the urban world of large towns: the workers and, above all, the 'upstarts'. This was the word that said it all.

Among 'my' bourgeois, clothing fully expressed those customs and traditions. It was affected by numerous prohibitions, in particular where colours were concerned. In the early sixties, the aunts of one of my seaside friends, penniless bourgeoises from an old family of Breton naval officers, on several occasions commented in my presence on the lapses in taste that a 'nice' young man should avoid. The most serious concerned trousers: never, never, never should trousers be of a darker colour than one's jacket or pullover. As for ties, they should never be worn with a white shirt, never be more pale than the shirt and never be anything but uniform in colour – for example, striped or a version of some tartan. Even spotted ties were banned. For it to be acceptable for a young man to shed his jacket, which was, in itself, tolerated in hot weather, two conditions had to be observed. Firstly, he should be wearing beneath the jacket a long-sleeved shirt, not a short-sleeved one; and secondly, he should also remove his tie. Whatever the circumstances, for all garments a single-coloured material was preferable to a patterned one; at a pinch, stripes were acceptable, but they should be thin and unobtrusive: if the stripes on his suit or shirt were wider, even very slightly wider, that was enough to turn a well-brought-up young man into the son of a *Mafioso*. Furthermore, brown – all shades of brown – should be banned except during the autumn months. Blue was better. But it should never be worn over red and red should never be worn over blue: that would be vulgar. As for jeans, they were not ruled out but had to be worn with a pale blue shirt and a navy-blue pullover. Never should jeans be accompanied by a jacket, even a sports-jacket, although a nautical jacket might, at a pinch, be acceptable.

That priority granted to the colour blue, whether pale or dark, puts me in mind of a remark that my father and his Surrealist friends discovered in a plea made in 1934 in favour of a particular uniform by a preacher who was the head of a well-known college for young people: 'When pale blue is found in association with navy-blue, the two form a pair of colours that steers the pupils away from bad thoughts.' Such a declaration filled them with delight; just as I rejoiced at an expression used by my friend's aunts, mentioned above. According to them, when it came to clothes, one should always aim for a 'neutral shade in good taste'. What could 'a neutral shade in good taste' possibly be? Were the two terms even compatible? After all, once all that we like, feel, react to, detest or think is seen through other people's eyes, what exactly can 'neutral' mean? Roland Barthes, who addressed this subject in his last course of lectures at the Collège de France, died before he could tell us. But the lecture notes that he left suggest that he had found himself a subject that was vast, complex and extremely fascinating.

MITTERAND BEIGE

The first time that I encountered the expression 'Mitterand beige' was in a novel by Frédéric Dard, in his San Antonio series. His mascot-hero, Alexandre-Benoit Béruvier, who helped to bring in sales of more than 500,000 copies, wore a raincoat described as 'Mitterand beige', which, as often happens, was spattered with grease spots. Later, in the early nineties, I again came across this expression, used in other contexts and by different authors. It was a purely chromatic expression with no political overtones or any slangy or popular connotations, let alone journalistic ones; an authentically literary expression, almost scholarly and truly splendid.

I do not know whether Frédéric Dard was responsible for it, although I do know that he was close to the president (which, however, did not stop him being critical of him). But I am almost certain that the expression alluded to the colour of a summer suit that François Mitterand wore for at least two seasons. It was a lightweight linen or cotton suit, not very well cut and a shade of beige that certainly did not become him. The former president was not, in fact, well adapted to smart, official clothes, especially those that were designed for the summer. Dressed in tweed or corduroy, he looked sturdy and imposing; but in suits that were too pale and too lightweight he became awkward and ridiculous. It is strange that his fashion-advisers did not notice this or take it into account. Why, in the warm summer months, did they dress up an ageing president in a beige suit, when a simple navy one would have been a thousand times more unassuming and appropriate? Was François Mitterand averse to navy-blue? Or, if not he, perhaps his entourage was. Was navy-blue naively – and stupidly – regarded in the Elysée Palace as too serious, too classical, too 'right-wing'? How, when one is an expert on appearances and communications, can one make such mistakes? When clad in beige, the president seemed at one and the same time badly turned out in his Sunday best, in which he looked more than his age, and as if he was tired of no longer believing in his own values.

In truth, the shade of that beige was disastrous: both too pale and too flashy, like that of some petty provincial miscreant, and with a suggestion of mouldy mustard that was really unpleasant. To be sure, I had only ever seen that suit in photographs or on television, so could not judge its true material quality. Besides, was it always the same suit or were there several of them, all cut from the same cloth? How many copies of a single suit does a president of the Republic possess? Shall we ever know? In any case, the shade of that beige always seemed identical: a nasty beige at once out of date yet too new; a provincial beige or the beige of some shady district; a vulgar beige like something out of a 1940s novel, clumsily reintroduced as fashionable after excessively thorough treatment at the cleaners. In short, a 'Simenon beige' that had become a 'Mitterand beige'. It had nothing, absolutely nothing, to do with the splendid aristocratic beiges worn by my favourite author, Vladimir Nabokov, at the end of his life, on the shores of Lake Geneva, where I had on several occasions spotted him without daring to approach him (probably because I admired him too much).

Perhaps we shall one day learn how much that horrible 'Mitterand beige' cost the Left in terms of votes in the early 1990s.

SLIMMING COLOURS

'He would have been simply corpulent had he not been so fat' ('*Tantum optimus nisi tam crassus*'). That is how Thomas Aquinas (died 1274) is humorously described by one of his biographers. The words are facetious, but neither ironical nor deprecating. In the thirteenth century, there was nothing demeaning about being fat. Happy days! All contemporary witnesses testified to the exceptional *embonpoint* of the great theologian. One of his disciples even went so far as to declare him 'the fattest man there ever was'. On this point, Thomas stands alongside Plato who, according to an ancient and recurring tradition, was said to be 'tall and very corpulent'. I confess to feeling a certain satisfaction knowing that two of the greatest of our Western thinkers were obese. Nowadays, it is so often assumed that a heavy body is incompatible with an agile mind . . .

Despite his corpulence, Thomas Aquinas was doubtless faced with no problems when it came to dressing himself. He wore a white Dominican robe, accompanied by a black cope to protect him from the cold and inclement weather. To be sure, the white of his robe emphasized his opulent figure more, probably, than the black of Benedictine vestments or the grey-brown of the Franciscan robe would have, but in those days his habit was the very mark of a monk or a priest; its colour even more so than the habit itself. Benedictines wore black, Cistercians white, Dominicans black and white, and Franciscans, who refused to dye wool and aimed for a most minimal degree of colour for their robes, were, despite their efforts, known by laymen as 'the grey friars'. A colour gave them their name. Later, Saint Francis of Assisi himself became 'Saint Grey' in a number of popular expressions. Hence the curse *'ventre-saint-gris'* (literally, 'Saint Grey's belly'), much used by Henry IV and still attested in the mid seventeenth century. It was a more or less obscene exclamation, meaning something like 'By the bowels of Saint Francis'.

Today, for a corpulent person, finding clothes to fit is a difficult and painful business, as I, after decades of experience, know all too well. As a child, I was not fat; I became so when I reached puberty, and remained so until I was about 18. Then I lost weight. Between the ages of 18 and 35, my weight remained that of a normal man. But after that I gradually grew fatter, putting on an average of 2 kilos each year, so that after twenty years I was 40 kilos overweight. Various diets resulted in my losing weight (in the course of my life I must have shed several hundred kilos!), but I clearly put it all, or even more, on again. On that account it has always been hard for me to tolerate being looked at, let alone to clothe myself.

In France, unlike in Germany and in the Netherlands, large sizes of ready-to-wear clothes for men soon run out (and in Italy, it is even worse). If one is too stout, one is obliged to resort to specialist establishments, gloomy little shops for 'big men', where the vocabulary used is certainly carefully controlled, but the scorn of the shop assistants is sometimes profound. A fat man is always at fault. But that is not the worst of it. What always disconcerts me in those shops for 'big men' is that it is so difficult to find garments in colours that are or are supposed to be 'slimming': black, grey or dark blue. No, what you are generally offered are jackets and trousers in pale colours, beiges, fawns, shades of green, pearly grey or else – as we have seen above – what is claimed to be navy-blue but isn't. It is as if a corpulent man is expected to come to terms with himself, scorn the glances of others and show that he is free and proud; in short, he is expected deliberately to choose shades that emphasize his overweight body. But instead of this experience being liberating and engendering a sense of pride and well-being, it feels like a punishment, even a humiliation, as I well know. And the range of colours offered for summer-wear is even more 'fattening' than those for the autumn or winter: white, sky-blue, pale green, yellow, even pinks and oranges. The cruelty of the producers of clothes knows no bounds!

Proof of this is provided by mail-order catalogues. Some of them, the best-known, offer a special supplement or booklet for 'large sizes'. The prices are certainly lower than those in the shops catering for 'big men', but the range of colours, fabrics and patterns is distressing: light shades, floppy fabrics, horizontal stripes and garish patterns. Wearing them, a corpulent man can be spotted from 100 yards away. Who are the designers or dictators of fashion who decide on such clothing for people who suffer from their *embonpoint* and who are solely bent on wearing clothes that are dark and as subdued and neutral as possible? Are they marketing specialists who are totally incompetent? Inhibited stylists seeking attention? Malevolent promoters? Scrawny fellows out for revenge?

IN THE LONDON UNDERGROUND

London, the autumn of 2004. It is raining. I had come to the British Museum, to study once more the famous medieval chess pieces found on the Isle of Lewis. But the curator with whom I had arranged to meet was not there. So three hours of freedom lay before me. As the weather ruled out taking a walk, I decided to visit a Somerset House exhibition devoted to the history of the London Underground. The display was low-key and consisted mostly of photographs. To my great surprise, some of these were printed in colour as early as the 1930s, and by twenty years later this was common practice. From the 1970s onward, colour photographs became more numerous than black-and-white ones. They showed travellers at the ticket offices, on the stairs, in the corridors, on the platforms, on the trains. Their clothing was clearly visible and sometimes made it possible to distinguish one social class from another.

For a historian, such photographs constitute precious documentation: these showed that, in the course of six or seven decades, the colours of clothes had changed very little. The cut of them had and so had the actual garments that made up a costume. But the colours had changed very little. In this context, it was not fashion that was displayed but everyday life, that is to say the garments that were actually worn by the people of London. Truly worn, not just photographed for magazines or shown in cinemas or on television. And throughout the 1940s, the 1960s, the 1980s and the 2000s, the colours were always the same. Always. Those that dominated were clearly black, grey, blue, beige and brown. White and green were rare, red even more so. As for yellow, purple, pink and orange hues, they were totally absent. For both sexes, all ages, all social categories and even all seasons, the range of colours remained unchanged. It is true that in London, the seasons, such as they were ... But I am sure that a similar exhibition devoted to the Paris *métro* would produce the same results.

We probably have a false idea of our clothes. We think that the pronouncements of fashion affect our choices, tastes and behaviour patterns. To a limited extent, that is true so far as shapes, lengths and combinations of garments go, and sometimes also the way that clothes are worn. But colours are not affected. You have only to observe people in the streets, in shops, in buses or in the *métro* to be struck by the general impression of chromatic uniformity. Everything is black, grey, brown, beige, white or blue. Rather more black and grey in the winter, and more blue and white in the summer. If anybody, usually a woman, wears red, yellow or purple, he or she stands out and attracts attention. Similarly, when we travel abroad, outside Europe, to the large towns of Asia, Africa or South America, it takes only a few seconds for the street scenes to show us how very different the range of clothing colours is from that of large European towns: it is brighter, more diverse, more confrontational.

Many reasons may be adduced to account for such differences. These may be of a historical, moral, social, material or even climatic nature. But two seem to me self-evident regarding the uniformity and constancy of European clothing. For one thing, nobody changes their wardrobe all at once. On the contrary, when we buy something new, we try to match it with whatever clothes we already possess – so colours change very little. Secondly, contrary to what some stylists and sociologists believe, the people who try not to call attention to themselves by their clothes greatly outnumber the rest.

I often think about the historians of the future, those who, in 200 or 300 years' time, will be studying the history of clothing in the early twenty-first century in Europe. Their stack of documentation will include our fashion magazines. But I hope that they will not be so naive as to think that, in 2010, we were really all dressed as the photographs of those magazines suggest. Nobody dresses like that in everyday life. The pictures reflect an imaginary representation of clothing, not the clothing that is really worn. It is a domain that may be just as interesting to study, but those are not photographs of everyday life. The same goes for the documentation that the past has left us. For example, the stained-glass windows, tapestries, miniatures, murals and other items of artistic evidence that have come down to us from the Middle Ages introduce us to many types of clothing, recording their nature, their forms and their colours. But we should not be so naive as to believe that the clothes really worn at such or such a date, in such or such a region and in such or such circles were identical to those displayed in stained-glass windows, tapestries and miniatures. For they were not. But nor were they altogether different. However, problems of documentation are not presented like that. Like language, images never convey reality completely faithfully. Certainly not the reality of colours.

2

DAILY LIFE

MY MOTHER'S PHARMACY

I grew up in Paris, in my mother's pharmacy, situated right at the top of Montmartre, opposite the water tower positioned in the middle of a little square. The pharmacy still exists and is probably the highest pharmacy in the Paris region. For the gang of children who lived at the top of Montmartre (about a dozen of us of roughly the same age), that square with its big tower constituted an inexhaustible playground, where we could play at processions, shout, argue, fight and play hide-and-seek. But my mother's pharmacy, facing on to the square, was quite different: calmer, more secretive and reserved for me. My parents never actually forbade me to play in the pharmacy, but they were not too keen on me inviting my playmates in. All the same, sometimes I did, for my parents were never particularly authoritarian. They were tolerant and favoured a bohemian lifestyle. They offered trust (and credit) to everyone, adults and children alike. That was no doubt why, when I was just 9 years old, my mother's business failed and we were obliged to leave Montmartre and settle in the southern suburbs, in an altogether different social, cultural and chromatic landscape.

In those days, in Paris, as elsewhere, every pharmacy was arranged as a place divided into zones carefully set out in a hierarchical order and organized by means of classifications and sub-classifications that were seldom altered. Colours played an essential role here, both in distinguishing between the various shelves and shelf-units and for identifying bottles, boxes and jars. In my mother's shop, for instance, the cupboard for dangerous substances, which I was never allowed to approach, was indicated by a red label bearing the word 'POISONS' in thick black letters. We called it 'the poison cupboard'. The combination of red and black, a coupling of colours that was more aggressive and expressive than any other, had the effect of making this off-limits cupboard more visible than all the rest. Upon entering the pharmacy, you saw it alone, which was presumably quite the opposite of what was intended.

Medicaments and their packaging were less eye-catching. More subtle too. Even in those days, in a shop, dispensary or workshop, nothing was labelled more carefully, more fastidiously or more subtly than a box of medicaments. That is still the case today, or even more so. Pharmaceutical laboratories invest considerable sums in the design and production of such containers. No other type of products – not even perfumes or cosmetics – is subject to such rules and is packaged, presented and labelled with such care. On the boxes containing medicaments, colour plays a moderate but carefully judged role. White is the dominant colour, conferring upon the boxes an aspect at once hygienic, scientific and beneficent – for white stands for both knowledge and purity. Often, the letters of the texts indicating the name of the product, that of its producer and the dosage are printed not in black, for against the white background the contrast would be too sharp and aggressive, but in grey. Nowadays, it is probably on this packaging for medicaments, or at least on some of it, that the most attractive and delicate range of greys is to be found. Here and there, a few splashes of colour may draw attention to the laboratory logo and, in accordance with a tacit but effective code, indicate the nature or function of the product contained in the box. A range of blues is used to label sedatives, sleeping pills and stress-relieving products. In contrast, yellow and orange shades are used for tonics, vitamins and products designed to increase energy and dynamism. Sometimes a rainbow sequence of colours – with blues removed! – may be used for those same products. In contemporary Western perception, orange tones and polychrome series, the colour of the sun and those of the rainbow, are more or less synonymous, for both are sources or signs of life. Beiges and browns tend to be reserved for medications that target digestion or the digestive system. But their presence on the box is muted: brown signifies a laxative only discreetly.

Green tones correspond to a variety of uses and medicaments (a fact that underlines the vast polysemy of this colour). In the past it was used relatively seldom (a residual effect of the old idea that green brought bad luck?). But today the vogue for ecology tends to make it the colour of mild medicines, of herbalist remedies and of numerous products of alternative medicine. As for black, it needs to be avoided altogether, for, clearly, under no circumstances should a medicament be associated with the colour of death. Even the abdominal charcoal remedies of my childhood, believed to relieve stomach or intestinal aches, were coded by some other colour (brown, yellow or pale purple). And then there is red, another colour that must be employed with caution. It may be used to evoke a taste, as in sweets (strawberry, raspberry, redcurrant), making it easier to wash down a pill or syrup given to children. Or it may codify an antibiotic or an antiseptic, on the strength of its relationship to blood and wounds. Also, and above all, however, it represents the colour of danger and prohibition, as in the indispensable warning: 'Do not exceed the prescribed dose'.

Outside the shop, the cross that indicated my mother's pharmacy was green. In the 1950s, blinking neon lights were already available to draw attention to the crosses displayed by some pharmacies, but they were mostly reserved for opulent premises in fashionable quarters. My mother's pharmacy could not afford such luxury. It made do with a simple wooden cross painted dark green, a sign that was displayed by most of the pharmacies in Paris. Later, when I travelled to Italy for the first time, I noticed that the code was not the same throughout Europe: the pharmacy crosses in Italy were – and still are – red. This gave me the idea of an investigation into the history of such emblems that are linked both to health and to commerce.

In the Middle Ages, green was already the emblematic colour for apothecaries, given that the pharmacopeia was in those days mostly drawn from the world of plants. Nevertheless, up until the mid nineteenth century, apothecaries used a variety of signs for their shops (animal horns, images of healer-saints and so forth). In France, it was not until the 1880s that the first green crosses made their appearance, prompted by a ruling according to which pharmacists of many towns were required to signal their premises by one specific sign. That cross now evoked the idea of aid, care and assistance. It was already to be seen on the clothing worn by the charitable religious orders established in the twelfth century to assist Christian pilgrims making their way to Islamic territories. It also appeared on the coats of arms of numerous charitable institutions under the Ancien Régime. And it was the sign adopted as the emblem of the Red Cross by the Geneva Convention of 1863–4. The influence of the Swiss flag – a white cross on a red background – no doubt also affected the choice of this emblem. The Italian pharmacies conformed to that model and use it to this day. They prefer the colour of blood to that of pharmacopeia and the idea of care and bandages to that of drugs, potions and herbal remedies.

It is worth noting that, in France, over the past twenty years, a number of pharmacies have replaced their green crosses by blue ones or blue-and-green ones. The change was certainly not gratuitous (where emblems are concerned, signs are never arbitrary; they also have a motive), even if the reasons for it are hard to discern. Was it a matter of extending the blue of charitable hospices, given that French hospitals, as institutions, tended to adopt that colour as their emblem (generally in association with white)? Or was it a way of declaring that the modern pharmacy is 'a space of wellbeing', a place of consultation and learning – notions that are both symbolized by the colour blue – and that it is no longer a vulgar cavern of some herbalist, druggist or spice-connoisseur?

THE SAD TALE OF YOUNG PHILIPPE

My first journey abroad was to Switzerland, a country which, for a variety of reasons, has over the years become my second homeland. I was nine years old when I first discovered it. It was on the occasion of a winter-sports trip organized by the group of Wolf-Cubs (at that time known as a 'pack') to which I belonged. In truth, the place where we stayed was in the French Alps, in Haute Savoie, but it was only a few hundred metres distant from the Swiss frontier. We crossed that frontier every day, either on foot or on skis. In order to avoid possible hassles with the customs officials, the organizers of our little group had requested that every child should come equipped with an identity-card. Of course, none of us had until then possessed one. This was in the mid-fifties, a time when plenty of adults were likewise without one. In France, there was no rule according to which anybody was obliged to possess a national identity-card. My father, who was born in the Orne region in 1912 and died in that of Mayenne in 1996, had passed the whole century without any identity documents, not even a driving licence. Happy man! Happy times!

In 1956, the business of acquiring a national identity-card resembled an assault course, particularly for a child. He had to present himself at the town hall in school hours, accompanied by one of his parents and equipped with various documents that were hard to obtain. He then had to fill in questionnaires with lots of tiny boxes, know how to sign with a proper signature, submit to the repugnant procedure of finger-printing without messing everything up and, most importantly, supply identification photographs that were 'in conformity with the regula-tions'. Obtaining those photographs was by no means easy. It is true that machines of the automatic photography booth type did already exist, but they were few and far between and, like telephone boxes, were almost always out of order. Furthermore, they produced photographs in which everyone, adults and children alike, resembled ex-convicts. It was on this account that some families opted to apply to a professional photographer for photographs of their children. It was more expensive but the results were closer to their expectations.

That was what the family of my classmate Philippe did. He, like me, was a Wolf-Cub in the Saint-Lazare pack. I knew him well for we both belonged to the same 'sixer' of six Wolf-Cubs, but I did not like him. He was a 'show-off', very sure of himself, whose parents were wealthy and let you know it. There was even a television in his home, which in 1956 was a sign of considerable wealth (these days, that is no longer the case). For this famous identity-card, his father, no doubt just as much of a show-off as his son, had had him photographed in colour, a rare procedure in those days. Philippe was proud of his photos and brought them to Wolf-Cub meetings on three consecutive Thursdays, making a great, pushy fuss of exhibiting them. He was the only one amongst us to possess such treasures. We were jealous, for we could only produce ordinary black-and-white photos. Those colour photos of our classmate, looking much too well-behaved in his Sunday best, seemed to us both wonderful and, at the same time, an insulting affront, a *narguerie*, a word much in vogue among schoolboys at that time. And Philippe did indeed affront us with his splendid, insufferable photos.

But we were soon avenged. His father was late in organizing his son's identity-card; and when, about ten days before our departure for winter-sports, the two of them turned up at the town hall, the civil servant in charge rejected the famous colour photographs. They were, he claimed, unacceptable because they were in colour. The father lost his temper and threatened to bring the influence of invented important figures to bear. But it was all to no avail. The photographs would have to be taken again, this time in black-and-white. There were more dramas, followed by a total collapse, for the business dragged on for several days and the identity-card was not ready in time. Philippe did not accompany us to winter sports and so did not discover Switzerland that year. Not knowing the cause of his absence, we thought he must be ill and even felt quite sorry for him. Not too much though. It was only much later, upon our return, that we learnt of the juicy fate of the colour photos and, with the cruelty of nine- and ten-year-olds, mocked our nasty little classmate. For several weeks, his pride prevented him from returning amongst us.

The sad tale of young Philippe is less anecdotal than it seems. It underlines the degree to which, fifty years ago in France, colour photography was still regarded as something suspect and inaccurate. Not only was official and legal documentation expressed in black-and-white, but that was also the case for everything exact, serious, accurate and true. Colours were reserved for frivolity, anything picturesque, leisure-time and even pleasure and debauchery. Admittedly, colour photography had not yet acquired the qualities that it manifests today, including in the domains of cutting-edge science.

In the course of one half-century, practices, techniques, codes and value-systems have certainly changed; it is now obligatory to produce colour photographs in order to obtain most identification documents; and those photos, furthermore, must respect extremely stringent rules concerning format, framing and the viewing angle. Even smiling is forbidden, which certainly says something about present-day society . . . As for black-and-white, considered in the past to be truer and more precise, it is nowadays considered inadequate and less faithful. Not everywhere, however: there are still organizations that insist that candidates for employment provide a CV accompanied by black-and-white photos. Their numbers are dwindling though – at least in France they are, while in Germany they remain in the majority.

Such oppositions between colour and black-and-white are not new. They first appeared toward the end of the fifteenth century, when engraved images, printed in black ink upon white paper began to be widely diffused. The introduction of engravings represented a veritable revolution in comparison to the images of the medieval period, which almost always incorporated several colours. In the world of the arts, particularly that of painting, such controversies were at the heart of debates which, throughout the following two centuries, set in sometimes violent opposition those who supported the primacy of drawing against those who considered colour images to be superior. The former were even then arguing that colour was a useless artifice, an over-beguiling cosmetic, a deception that altered forms, abused the view of spectators and distracted them from what was essential. The latter declared that colour alone made it possible to attain to the truth of beings and things and that the effects and endeavours of painting were primarily linked with colour. Later, we shall see why it is that I have enlisted in the camp of the latter.

SWEET DISPENSERS

I was a greedy, spoilt child who, in the course of the decade prior to adolescence, must have consumed a quantity of confectionery that would normally suffice for ten children of his age. Later, of course, I paid for this.

In Paris in the 1950s, every trip in the *métro* afforded me a chance to 'draw' a packet of sweets from the dispenser provided in the middle of the platform. Such dispensers were not to be found in every station, only in around one-third of them, especially ones where one could switch to a different line. One such was Raspail, the station at which I left the train when visiting my grandmother. At the foot of the Montmartre hill, however, there were no confectionery dispensers in the stations that my parents used: namely, Abbesses and Lamark-Caulincourt. At

Anvers, another station where we sometimes took the *métro*, there was a dispenser, but only on one platform and it was not the usual colour: it was grey instead of orange. Why only one platform? And why grey?

As I recall, these dispensers were almost everywhere painted orange, a colour considered to evoke delicacies, arouse desire and brighten up life. Later, in the seventies, the colour orange was used to a naive, immoderate and altogether ineffective degree: how could a shade of orange brighten up life? Most of the dispensers of my childhood were quite narrow and offered only four varieties of sweets in four different kinds of packaging; others, dazzlingly new, were wider and offered six kinds. All these sweets were enclosed in little cardboard boxes, which landed in a curved receptacle once you had inserted a yellow 20-franc coin and pulled the heavy metal lever positioned in the middle of the dispenser. The descent of the box of sweets was accompanied by a booming noise that echoed round the whole station, attracting all eyes to the generous machine, in particular the envious looks of children whose parents refused to buy them such junk.

My favourite sweets were filled with what claimed to be mandarin syrup. They were little balls, coloured orange and rounded like the fruit itself and they contained a sugary liquid that, to me, tasted exquisite. What percentage of genuine mandarin juice could that nasty syrup really have contained? Probably none at all. But I didn't care. I found those sweets delicious and they helped to pass the time of the journey, for they were hard and you had to suck them for a long time before you could reach that precious liquid. To be deprived of it seemed, as I saw it, a serious and unfair punishment.

I remember all this very clearly, in particular the orange colour of the dispensing machines. However, a few years ago, while leafing through a number of works on the history of the Paris *métro*, I came across several photos showing the platforms – strangely deserted – in the 1950s, the years of my childhood. Some of them were even in colour. There they were, those famous confectionery dispensers, in the middle of the platforms, narrow and upright, like petrol pumps; but they were not orange: some were a yellowy-beige, others just unpainted, vaguely silvery metal. Why such a wide discrepancy between the colour that I remembered and the colours that these documents showed? Were the photos wrongly dated and really five or ten years later than they were labelled as being? Or were the *métro* stations shown exceptional ones that harboured sweet dispensers of an unusual colour and thus conveyed to posterity information that was at odds with the general situation. A historian is well aware that documentation, for whatever period, often plays such tricks: whatever is unusual is easier to preserve and transmit than what is usual.

All the same, would it not make more sense to admit that my memory deceived me, this memory in which I tend to place too much faith just because it allows me effortlessly to recall dozens of telephone numbers, endless lists of sporting results and hundreds (even thousands?) of dates linked with historical events. Does it deceive me in my own special field of research, namely that of colour? Perhaps. This was not the first time that I had found it wanting on some point to do with colour. Had I, in this particular case, confused a part with the whole? Had I projected onto the sweet dispensers the colour of the sweets themselves? The fact is that I do not remember ever having obtained from these dispensers anything other than those round, sugary, garishly orange mandarin-flavoured sweets. So had I, in my memories, coated the machines themselves in the colour orange?

Where colours are concerned it is, as we shall see, relatively common to confuse one part for the whole.

CHOOSING A COLOUR: AN IMPOSSIBLE UNDERTAKING?

I am not keen on driving and am not particularly attracted to cars. To tell the truth, it is not so much the vehicles themselves that exasperate me, but all the posturing that surrounds them. How can one be proud of possessing a big car? Of driving fast? Of showing off behind the wheel? Those are infantile, ridiculous ways of behaving. In a car, the most important thing for me is the colour of the bodywork. Nor am I alone in prioritizing this aspect. Various opinion polls conducted in the last five decades show that not only was colour one of the important criteria when choosing a car to buy but it was, after the price, in some cases the most important criterion of all. For some customers, more of them than might be supposed, what mattered more than the make, the model, the car's performance or any other feature was the car's colour. Bewildered by such a revelation, the makers of cars at first decided to ignore it. Later, succumbing to the pressure of demand, they were led somewhat to reconsider their policy where the colour-range was concerned and to take more account of the wishes of the public and the whims of fashion. But they did so rather reluctantly, even with some repugnance. For engineers and technicians, the colour of the body-work was insignificant, the more so as, on the production-line, the task of painting a car was the last to be undertaken. Only car salesmen recognize (or ought to) the importance of colour for their sales technique. But in the automobile industry, their activities are far from being considered as the primary sector.

The importance that people attach to colour is nothing new. As early as the start of the twentieth century, the majority of clients were enamoured of colour while most car-manufacturers were averse to it, emulating Henry Ford (1863–1947), the founder of the Ford Motor Company. Despite the desires of the public, despite the two-tone or three-tone vehicles offered by certain competitors and despite the growing place of colour in everyday life, this idiosyncratic and anti-Semitic Puritan always, for what he considered to be moral reasons, refused to sell cars that were other than black, or mainly black: the famous Ford T, the star that his company produced from 1908 to 1927, in itself symbolized that rejection of colour.

Despite my lack of interest in cars, I have, in my lifetime, bought several: at first, second-hand ones, but later, new ones – an infrequent operation but a challenging one, as it required me to confront mechanics and all that technical discourse of theirs that is so obscure to ordinary mortals.

The discourse is obscure but it may be instructive, particularly for a historian of colours. In the eighties I thus came to appreciate the particular status enjoyed by red cars, which were relatively rare in France. Wishing to buy a second-hand vehicle, I was lucky enough to benefit from a bargain price because I had chosen a 'family car' the body-work of which was red. The car-salesman told me that this model was one that appealed to elderly people, set in their ways, who were not at all interested in speed or competitive performances but who did dislike this car's red colour: it was too bright, too eccentric, too 'fast'. Meanwhile, younger clients, who might have been attracted by this aggressive and dynamic colour, considered the model too 'dated' and the engine too low-key. The vehicle thus seemed unmarketable unless the buyer was offered an enticingly low price. And so the deal was done.

Up until recent times, red cars were bound to be fast cars. The colour of the Ferraris that took part in Formula I races provided (and still provide) their emblematic image. Likewise, on motorways one never encountered a red car that was being driven in a laboured manner. Such a car was in duty bound to go fast. The situation was such that, up until the 1970s, certain insurance companies in France demanded special rates from the owners of red cars: not because they were red but because, being red, they would be driven by youthful drivers – that is to say, drivers reckoned to be more accident-prone than most. Such practices, common only one generation ago, today seem unbelievable and so arbitrary as to be the subject of heated polemics. Some insurance companies will even deny that they ever existed. But they are wrong.

Be that as it may, to choose the colour of one's car at the moment when one buys it is almost an impossibility, even if the car is a new one. Of course, the salesman will produce a variegated colour-chart, showing a range of very attractive shades. But in reality the possibilities of making a real choice are limited: one colour will not be available for six months, another is more expensive, yet another is not available for this particular model or is incompatible with some other option. So the client's choice is reduced to three or four shades. He rules out those he dislikes and ends up choosing not a colour for which he has a positive liking, but the one that he dislikes the least of those that are on offer – which is not at all the same thing. Still today, truly choosing the colour of one's car remains a purely theoretical dream. On that very account, the scholarly conclusions that sociologists sometimes draw when producing statistics that relate to the colours most preferred for cars in particular regions, particular countries, particular decades and particular social circles remain questionable. The figures arrived at reflect not so much the real preferences of the public – rather, a lack of imagination, bad taste, moral nostalgia or a childish craving for innovation on the part of the car-makers.

Like it or not, though, we are all judged, classified, represented by statistics and described on the basis of the colours of our cars – and many other objects and practices too, starting with our clothes. But that colour hardly ever corresponds to our deepest tastes and seldom reflects the image that we would like to convey of ourselves. It really is quite scandalous. A car with bright, unusual colours suggests that one is an unsteady and aggressive driver; a red car proclaims a madman at the wheel; a black one indicates an austere person or some official figure. White cars and yellow ones are considered more feminine; green ones are younger; brown, mustard-coloured or orange ones are in bad taste. Shades of grey, on the other hand, are considered understated and elegant. At least, that is the way it was in France in 2010. In Germany, Italy and the Scandinavian countries, the connotations attached to the range of colours used for the body-work of cars were different. In France itself, colours that indicate sensitivity today did not do so twenty years ago and will no doubt be obsolete in five or ten years' time. Colour symbolism is always cultural. It varies from one place to another and changes with time. Moreover, it may go into reverse or break the rules so that it arrives at new value-systems. Driving a car that is pink or purple when one is an honest family man or a respectable country lawyer may be a way of showing that one is so honest or so respectable that one can indulge in the luxury of flouting the code.

GREYNESS

My first visit to a country living under a Communist regime took place somewhat late, in 1981. I was already over thirty years old and had for several years been working on the history of colours. It was in order to attend a series of colloquia and lectures that I travelled beyond the Iron Curtain for the first time, to East Germany. Although tension remained high between the two blocs, various Western garments and products had already found their way to the larger towns of East Germany, in particular to East Berlin. However, despite the timid nature of this breakthrough, what struck me most on that first trip was not the inflexibility of the university world, nor the Spartan nature of most hotels, nor, even less, the tone of the exchanges in the course of various encounters in which the views expressed were in many cases positivist or reflected wishful thinking. What impressed me most deeply and most painfully was the sight of the streets. The colour in the air bore no relation to what was to be seen in the West, which itself was not nearly as many-coloured as emergent or third-world countries.

There, in the large towns of East Germany, everything, or almost everything, was either grey or brown: not necessarily old, dirty or down-at-heel, but a sad grey or a dull – as it were, dead – brown. It is true that a few large splashes of bright colours, here or there, were supposed to brighten the lives of passers-by and inhabitants, but they were much too violent, more of an aggression than a comfort. Similarly, while most items of clothing were in shades of brown, a few did aim to be modern, but favoured garish colours and excessively gaudy patterns. The sober, unpatterned colours and subdued stripes that were generally considered to be in good taste in Western Europe were almost unknown. It was not that everything was poverty-stricken, but it all seemed gloomy, weary and vulgar. It was the more depressing because a Western visitor received the impression that the manufacturers and industrialists of East Germany could very well have invented and produced a smarter ambience without spending any more money or changing their methods.

In this respect, one particular shade that I had noticed several times in the Berlin underground or in the streets of Jena and Leipzig seemed to me to be typical. Up until then, I had never come across it. It was used for numerous items of clothing – both masculine and feminine (raincoats in particular) – the façades of buildings, a variety of objects for daily life and a number of means of transport (bikes, cars, trucks). It is not easy to find words to describe it. It was not, strictly speaking, just a purplish brown, rather a shade somewhere between brown, grey and purple with (and this is perhaps the most remarkable thing about it) a slight tinge of greenish yellow as if, as a finishing touch, there had been an attempt to add a hint of 'mustard' to this revolting colour. In the West it would have been hard to produce such a colour and impossible to sell it. Disagreeable to the eye and wounding to the soul, it was as ugly as could be and, on top of everything, there was something brutal and uncivilized about it that appeared to stem from the most uncouth codes of social life, a kind of *Urfarbe* (original colour) inherited from the barbaric times of the first industrial revolution and resistant to all modernity. I remember wondering how the chemistry of colouring agents in Communist countries managed to produce such a nuanced shade. What materials were used, what recipes were followed and, above all, with what aim? It was not a specifically German shade, more of a Communist one, for later on I also came across it in Poland. Was it easier to obtain it using pigments and colouring agents that were cheap? Was one of its advantages that it did not show the dirt? In truth, it did look dirty right from the start.

Since the fall of the Berlin Wall, a whole commemorative process has been set in place in the former East Germany, its purpose being to preserve the memory of those years spent under the Communist regime. Some of the memories are of a nostalgic nature and are evoked not only by literature and the cinema but also by certain items that have become cult objects or museum pieces. Nowhere, however, have I ever found any trace in any museum of the purplish, mustard-tinged greyish brown that seemed to me so characteristic of that *ancien régime*. No doubt such a nuanced shade, so painful, almost inhuman, turned out to be impossible to mythologize.

MÉTRO TICKETS

The underground is a particularly good place for observing numerous codes and patterns of behaviour involving colour. As I have already pointed out, it is in the underground that an observer is presented with the sight of the range of clothing colours truly worn by the people of large towns. It is there that one is best placed to appreciate the sometimes huge gap between everyday colours in which ordinary people dress and the imaginary and unwearable colours of the garments photographed in fashion magazines. Perhaps stylists, fashion designers and sociologists should take the underground more often. In this subterranean place, signalling by means of colour plays an important role – more important than it does on trains or planes. On the maps which help travellers to find their way and which, on account of the plethora of indications that they have to provide, abide by an elaborate code of cartography, the use of colour is the most effective way of distinguishing between the various underground lines. Many underground users, particularly in Anglo-Saxon countries, pick out each line on the map by means of a particular colour, not by its name or number. It would be interesting to know, in the cases of large towns, when and why a particular colour was assigned to a particular line (I seldom think that such signs are arbitrary), and then to study the symbolism that has developed over the decades.

Similarly, the history of the colouring of *métro* tickets – items now on the way out – has yet to be written. In my own lifetime in Paris, I have known reddish tickets and yellowish ones which, in the 1950s, distinguished between the First and the Second classes. Then I witnessed all the tickets becoming beige, which for a long time they remained. The Parisian transport authorities described this colour as 'Havana yellow'! A little later, in the 1970s, yellow tickets made their appearance, with a brown magnetic band on the reverse side. Then came *chic et choc* tickets, promoted by a publicity campaign as strident as it was futile. Punched holes in tickets were a thing of the past; they were no longer clipped. In 1992, those yellow tickets turned green, a shade of green verging on turquoise that the administration of the Parisian transport authority pompously described as 'jade green'. The change in colour affected not only the basic ticket, valid for a single journey, but all tickets, including a weekly one which, up until then, had been a 'Havana yellow', slightly paler than the rest. To make it more easily identifiable, this weekly ticket carried the words COUPON JAUNE (Yellow Coupon) printed in bold letters on the card. When, in 1992, all tickets became jade green, this one did likewise, yet for several months the inscription 'Yellow Coupon' remained. This object that was now green formally proclaimed itself to be 'yellow'! Its actual colour and its stated colour were strangely different.

But in truth perhaps this was not all that strange. Without realizing, we use this or that colour-term to qualify objects whose colouration has little to do with the word used. For example, day in, day out, we speak of 'white wine' when referring to wine that is not white at all. Similarly, we use the word 'red' to qualify wine that in truth is not red; we call purple grapes 'black' and grapes that are a greenish yellow 'white'. This in no way bothers us, given that our ancestors and their ancestors too did likewise from times immemorial. Perhaps even from the time of Noah.

The discrepancies between real colours and those used as the names of products in daily usage that have a strong symbolic character, like wine, remind us of the extent to which colours are above all a matter of conventions, labels and social codes. Their primary function is to differentiate, classify, associate, oppose and establish hierarchies. In Europe, wine and grapes were allotted their colour-labels way back in ancient times, when only three colours – white, red, and black – were required. Of course, other colours did exist, but in codes and value-systems they played no more than a minor role. It would not make much sense to say that a wine was yellow or a grape was purple. Describing these items as 'white', 'red' or 'black' conferred upon them a truly poetic or symbolic dimension, which they have preserved right down to the present day.

RED OR BLUE?

Let us remain on our seats in the underground, or rather in the RER [Réseau Express Régional]. I would now like to put on record a comment on the behaviour of travellers on this rail network that may appear anecdotal but in truth underlines the fact that colour is never neutral; it is always charged with an ideological dimension which, far more than its claimed physiological effects, conditions both our choices and our attitudes.

In the southern suburbs of Paris, in the early 1980s, the B line of the RER (formerly the *ligne de Sceaux*) was supplied with new carriages in which red seats alternated with blue ones. This made a change from the gloomy greens and browns of former days and those responsible for the change assumed that the effect would be to cheer up these communal means of transport: worthy enough intentions – worthy but naive.

Not long after the appearance of these new carriages (new, but not for long), I noticed that at uncrowded times, that is to say when travellers were free to choose where they would sit, virtually nobody went to sit on the red seats. It was as if this colour – the colour of danger and prohibition, but also that of festivity and love – was off-putting, alarmed people, seemed unsuitable or at least less neutral than blue. Unfortunately, I failed at the time to seize the opportunity to observe the fearless travellers who, in these uncrowded hours, were brave enough to park their bottoms on the red seats: were they young, were they rebels, were they well-heeled people unaccustomed to travelling on the RER, or were they colour-blind? Such an enquiry would doubtless have been of sociological interest. So the fact that the opportunity was lost is all the more regrettable since by now the wear-and-tear, dirtiness and dilapidation of the said seats sometimes makes it difficult for an observer or for an ordinary traveller to see whether the seat is blue or red. We shall have to wait for the seats to be replaced once more by new ones, at which point we should waste no time in assessing dirtiness and vandalism in order to produce a proper ethnology of the colours used in public transport. (But will those new seats still be red and blue?)

TRAFFIC LIGHTS

When were red, amber and green lights first used in towns for traffic control? This was a question that I tried to answer about thirty years ago, when I was working on the origins of the highway code and the role that colours played in it. Serious research in this domain was uncommon and reliable documentation was more or less non-existent. Having failed to find any relevant information in the Bibliothèque nationale or in the national archives, I had the idea of paying a visit to the library of the Department of Bridges and Roads (*Ponts et Chaussées*), thinking that there I might find specialized studies on this subject, in particular certain German articles published in the inter-war years in journals that were hard to find.

This library, then situated in Paris in the rue des Saints-Pères, was undergoing renovation work and I was directed to an annexe out in the suburbs. My efforts to make use of it were disappointing. I could find nothing in the reference books, nothing in the filing system. Overcoming my shyness, I turned to the librarian on duty in the reading room and explained my subject of research. He looked alarmed, asked me to repeat my request, then summed it up in a questioning manner: 'The history of red lights?' I specified that I was working more generally on the beginnings of urban traffic lights in Europe and the United States. This seemed to upset him even more. He told me he would have to consult a colleague, who was seated at another desk at the other end of the reading room and was possibly his superior officer in the library hierarchy. My eyes followed him and I saw the two men exchange a few words, shoot a suspicious glance in my direction, then

resume their conversation. Eventually, the second librarian brought it
to a close, placing an index finger against his brow and twisting it this
way and that, probably to indicate that I was some dotty reader, working on a ridiculous subject and wasting their time. I expect I had come
on a bad day.

I left the *Ponts et Chaussées* library – or rather, its temporary annexe
– empty-handed but confirmed in my sense of how difficult it was to
get those around me to understand that the history of colours is not
a totally futile subject to study. It was not the first time that I had
encountered incomprehension from an acquaintance, relative, friend,
colleague or student. At best, the history of colours was considered to
belong to 'minor history', collections of anecdotes and *curiosa*; at worst,
it indicated that the mind of anyone dabbling in it was full of infantile,
obscure and despicable preoccupations. The situation in the 1880s, the
age of scientism and positivism, was certainly a far cry from the attitude
that prevailed in the 1980s, the period of semiology, the history of men-
talities and glorious multidisciplinarity!

A few years later, various spells of work in several German and
British libraries enabled me to retrace the broad lines of the history
of traffic lights and to discover that in numerous respects road-signals
were a legacy from the railway signals which, in their turn, had developed out of maritime signals that had been introduced in the eighteenth
century. On roads, as at sea, at first the lights were just two colours,
red and green. The earliest to be installed were those in London, in
December 1868, at the corner of Palace Yard and Bridge Street. The
mechanism consisted of a revolving gas-lamp, manoeuvred by a traffic
policeman. But the system was a hazardous one, for in the following
year an explosion fatally injured a constable who had come to light the
lamps. London nevertheless mainly led the way in this field. Paris only
followed suit in 1923 and Berlin did so in the following year. The first
Parisian traffic light was installed at the crossroads of the boulevards
Sébastapol and Saint-Denis. It was solely red. Not until the 1930s did
green lights appear. In the meantime, combinations of two coloured
lights had reached the United States: Salt Lake City in 1912, Cleveland
in 1914, New York in 1918.

Why were red and green the two colours chosen to control traffic,
first at sea, then for railways and finally for roads? Red had, of course,

been the colour for danger and prohibition ever since ancient times (already, more or less, in the Bible), but for many years green had nothing to do with permissions to proceed. On the contrary, it played the role of the colour of disorder, transgression and all that was contrary to the established rules and systems. Furthermore, it had not been regarded as an opposite to red as white had forever been, and as blue had been since half-way through the Middle Ages. But then, in the course of the eighteenth century, once the theories of Newton became known, the classification of colours changed. Newton had discovered the spectrum several decades earlier and, since that time, the scholarly world had become familiar with the opposition between primary colours and complementary ones. Now green was recognized as complementary to red, a primary colour. The two colours began to be paired together and, since red stood for prohibition, green, its complementary or almost opposite colour, gradually came to stand for permission. Between 1780 and 1840, at sea and then on land too, it became customary to 'give the green light' when authorizing traffic to proceed. A new history of colour codes was set in place. Green became the sign of permission to pass or even of freedom, as it has remained right down to the present day.

COLOUR AND DESIGN: A MISSED CHANCE?

Quite early on, colour introduced me into the world of fashion. With two or three major *couturiers*, various centres of style and several magazine directors, I was able to exchange certain ideas about fashion and colour symbolism. Sometimes we disagreed. For instance, I never considered a 'trend' to be an acceptable term to explain or justify a chromatic strategy. All the same, our exchanges were always fruitful. However, with the world of design and industrial creativity, my contacts came later and they were more limited. To tell the truth, they did not even begin until 1993, the year when a huge exhibition entitled 'Design, the Mirror of the Century' was organized in Paris, beneath the splendid glass of the Grand Palais. The organizers asked me to write an article for their catalogue, to be published under the same title by the Flammarion publishing house. The article was supposed to synthesize the relations between design and colour between the 1880s and the end of the twentieth century.

I knew very little about this subject. So I embarked on a full reading programme, questioned specialists and conducted a number of enquiries. To my great surprise, I found that, apart from the Bauhaus experience, colour had interested design specialists very little, whether they were creative designers, sociologists or historians. The silence maintained by the latter matches that of art-historians, who for long decades paid no attention at all to problems of colour (I shall be returning to this subject).

In the sector of industrial creativity, it was noticeable that, considered in the long term, design was hardly inventive at all in the domain of colours: colour symbolism was rudimentary, aesthetic theory was slack ('harmonize colour with the functions of objects') and the scene was dominated by a naive belief in a scientific truth about colours and in the optical and chemical laws that made it possible to control them.

Let us glance at a little history. What strikes one as one studies the mass-produced domestic articles of the late nineteenth and twentieth centuries is the uniformity of the limited range of colours used; almost all fall into a black, grey, white and brown range. Bright colours are rare. Why? The first answer that springs to mind is a need to investigate the chemistry of colouring agents: perhaps it was still too rudimentary to produce a large number of objects that were brightly coloured, true and diversified. In fact, though, that was not the case. Not only was European man in this period perfectly capable of producing, on an industrial scale, a particular shade decided upon in advance (a feat that, prior to the nineteenth century, he would have found it hard to achieve) but, furthermore, ever since the 1860s he had also been capable of multiplying such shades in profusion and using them to colour all kinds of objects.

In truth, the problem was neither one of chemistry nor one of technique; rather, it was of an ethical nature. The reasons why the first household appliances, fountain pens, telephones, cars and so on were black, grey, white or brown, and not orange, bright red or lemon yellow, were above all moral ones. For late nineteenth-century industrial society, bright colours, those that drew the eye and attracted attention, were improper and to be used sparingly. In contrast, more neutral and sober colours, within the grey/brown range or belonging to a black-and-white world, were considered to be dignified and worthy;

and so they should be mass-produced. For design in its early years, the
social morality of colours was thus a constraint that was hard to avoid.
The resistance with which this ethic opposed all attempts to rethink
the colour properties of objects was so strong that, following World
War I, the changes introduced into the range of available colours (now
brighter, truer and more varied) which appeared on the market, and
which were partly due to the artistic revolutions of the early twentieth
century, were dismissed by the general public as laughable, eccentric or
ridiculous commercial fantasies. They therefore remained marginal (a
fact that is not often emphasized) and were ignored by the culture of
the masses.

Subsequently, faith in science and the quest for 'chromatic truths'
accounted for design's simplistic attitude to colour. Seeking to balance the shapes, colours and functions of objects, design has until quite
recently believed in a natural, almost physiological quality of colour
– as if there really were pure colours and impure ones, warm colours
and cold colours, intimate colours and distancing ones, dynamic ones
and static ones, stimulating ones and calming ones. Forgetful of the
narrowly cultural character of colour symbolism, design has on several
occasions claimed to have created 'universal codes'. Not only do such
attempts now seem ridiculous but, more importantly, they have always
had the effect of alienating consumers, thereby foiling their initial aim:
namely, to harmonize both practical and aesthetic satisfaction. Not
everything to do with water can be blue; not everything to do with fire
can be red; not everything to do with nature can be green; not everything to do with sunshine and holidays can be yellow or orange. Not all
hospital rooms can be painted blue and white; not all fast cars are red;
not all children's toys are brightly and boldly coloured. Johannes Itten's
famous pronouncement, addressed to the students of the Bauhaus in
1922 but subsequently appropriated, for whole decades, by design, is
one of the most absurd ever written about colours: 'The laws of colour
are eternal, absolute, timeless, as valid in the past as they are today.'

The excessive credit granted to scientific theories has limited or
even misled the chromatic choices of industrial design. The case of
green is typical in this respect. First science, then contemporary art
(I am thinking of, for example, Mondrian and Dubuffet) denied it the
status of a primary colour, reducing it to the level of a complementary

one, somehow a secondary colour produced by mixing yellow and blue. This demoted status of green, which design was quick to accept, runs contrary to all traditions and customs. In this instance too, the public's sensibilities have been affronted, offended, even baffled.

A third factor that has limited the successes of industrial design where colour is involved is constituted by the phenomena of fashion. These are ephemeral, subtle and uncontrollable, not really individual but not collective either, and they stem from neither a psychological approach nor a simple sociological analysis. For a designer, producer and encoder of colours, the most difficult parameters to control are those that involve standing out or over-use. In the world of fashion (not just of clothing), a colour or a mixture of colours is only attractive and enhancing because it stands out from other colours or mixtures of colours: it breaks the mould, distances itself from tradition and all that is easily available, ubiquitous and abundant; and it does so not – as design would have it – because it is 'in harmony with the shape and function of whatever it is applied to'. Mass-production of this colour or this association of colours – which is the very purpose of industrial manufacture – will clearly condemn it to a lack of success or else to a no-more-than-fleeting success. In the fashion world, the scales tip one way or the other quickly and capriciously, for colours possibly even more than for other elements: when all cars were black, the last word in stylishness was the possession of a car that was red, blue or green; then, when all cars became brightly coloured, the ultimate was to have a grey car. The research of designers and the laws of mass-production have, so to speak, never been able to avoid this snare, which is all the more formidable and tortuous given that, in a single place and in the same period, every social circle, every age-group and every social or professional group or sub-group clings to its own values. And these are hard for an outsider to understand, impossible to channel, let alone to fix, and are ready to be reversed, to self-destruct or to undergo a metamorphosis at the slightest provocation.

This is why any historian is justified in claiming that nearly all the efforts that design makes to control or salvage the phenomena of fashion are doomed to failure or semi-failure. Real successes have only been made possible by perverting the aims and ethics of industrial production – for instance, by abandoning mass-production at the cost of low sales (the two fundamental constraints of true design) and by offering for sale domestic objects conceived from the start to be emblems of class, luxury articles. Swept up in the whirl of fashion cycles, economic laws and the vagaries of snobbishness, design – like other aspects of contemporary creativity – seldom emerges with increased stature from such an attitude. Raymond Loewy used to say, 'Ugliness does not sell well.' Quite true. But is not the creation of beauty simply in order to make money itself ugliness of a different kind?

EATING COLOURS

Once my enquiries into colour became somewhat known, I was on several occasions subjected to a painful ritual when invited out to dinner: the ritual of the monochrome meal. In an attempt to please me or to show off their know-how and ingenuity, my hosts would concoct for me a dinner in which all the dishes were designed around one particular colour. Sometimes the table arrangement would correlate with the colour of the food. Far from delighting me, this laborious setting perplexed me. Moreover, the slight pleasure afforded to the eye was hardly compensation for the absence of satisfaction for the mouth! The efforts involved in devising a meal in a single colour include making choices, links and combinations that certainly please the eye but that often detract from the taste. Colour and taste are different, whatever theories of synaesthesia may declare.

Actually, this fashion for single-coloured meals, which made a comeback in the 1980s, was by no means original. It had already appeared in the 1950s and had had a moment of glory even earlier, between 1910 and 1920, reflecting the influence of Futurist artists. In those days monochrome meals went hand in hand with an exaltation of modernity. Going further back in history, the forebears of such dinners could be found in banquets held in the later years of the Middle Ages (in which the food served was dyed in the colours of the arms or livery of the prince), and even earlier in the gastronomy of the Roman Imperial period. So there was nothing new about the tables of the bohemian bourgeois and imbibers of the late twentieth century.

Nor were they particularly inventive. Since 1980, many books of menus have been published for a readership of women (or men)

running a household and wishing to organize such meals. These books
all copied one another and never failed to point out how difficult it is
to devise a blue meal, for Nature provides very few foodstuffs that are
really blue. Purple, yes; black too; and red is even more common. But
blue? So it becomes necessary to cheat and to turn to the names of
foodstuffs or recipes rather than their true colours: *truite au bleu* or *bleu
des Causses* (a blue cheese). Another possibility is to dye white foodstuffs
(rice, pasta, hard-boiled eggs, celery, chicory, fish . . .) with blue meth-
ylene, a non-toxic product used in the past to soothe mouth ulcers and
nowadays for tinting the water of fish-tanks blue: on a plate, the shade
obtained is attractive and unexpected. In fact though there is no need
to resort to an artificial product of this kind, as it is perfectly possible
to use dyes of a variety of colours that are obtained from natural foodstuffs. Onion skins produce fine beige and light brown shades; spinach,
the juice of leeks, pistachio nuts and certain herbs produce excellent
greens; saffron gives an intense yellow; water in which artichokes are
cooked offers a magnificent blue-green; and cuttle-fish ink produces a
deep black. To obtain reds, pinks and purples, one is spoilt for choice:
use beetroot, red cabbage, blackcurrants, blackberries or bilberries.

Even without using natural colouring agents, devising a monochrome menu is not a problem except where shades of blue are concerned. Here are a few simple examples:

Red: beetroots, red tuna steaks, red beans, strawberries.
Orange: grated carrots, smoked haddock, pumpkin purée, a salad of
    oranges.
White: chicory salad, cod fillets, rice, white cheeses, litchis.
Green: cucumber salad, pesto tortellini, lettuce, a pistachio tart.
Brown: lentil salad, grilled beef, chestnut purée, chocolate mousse.
Black: lumpfish roe, tapenade, risotto with cuttle-fish ink, poppy-seed
    cake.

Artists, poets and novelists have preceded recipe books on this subject. For example, in *La Vie, mode d'emploi* (Instructions for Life), published in 1978, Georges Perec describes how a certain Madame Moreau
produces a single-coloured meal once a month in her white dining
room:

The first meal was yellow: chou pastry in the Bourguignon manner, pike dumplings with Hollandaise sauce; quail ragout with saffron, sweet-corn salad; lemon and guava sorbets, washed down with sherry, Chaton-Chalon, Chateau Carbonneux and an iced Sauterne punch.

Even more famous is the funeral meal described by Joris-Karl Huysmans (1848–1907) in his novel *À Rebours* (*Against Nature*) (1884). It is like a quotation from an anthology of Symbolist literature. In the course of the meal, served by 'naked negresses' in 'a dining-room draped in black' while an unseen orchestra plays funeral marches, all the food eaten is black, brown or purple, accompanied by beverages of those same colours:

> From black-edged plates, they had consumed turtle soups, Russian rye bread, ripe Turkish olives, caviar, mules' testicles, smoked black puddings from Frankfurt, giblets in a sauce the colour of liquorice and black shoe-polish, truffle jelly, scented chocolate creams, puddings, nectarines, fruit preserved in grape juice, blackberries and black cherries, accompanied by wines from Limagne, Rousillon, Tenedos, Val de Peñas and Port, quaffed from dark glasses. After coffee, walnut cordial, kvas, ports and stouts were enjoyed.

The monochrome menus served to me never attained such heights of affectation or of succulence. Of course, they had been served on plates, not in a book. I seldom enjoyed them, but I have known even worse: a meal entirely constructed around one single product. Not a plant, but an animal: it was torture! My works on the history and symbolism of pork gave a restaurant owner in Lyon the idea of inviting me to deliver a lecture on this subject in his own establishment and, to mark the occasion, of serving to 100 or more guests a luncheon entirely devoted to the pig. It was heavy and greasy, very heavy and very greasy. I would not wish upon anyone the obligation to consume the dessert served to us that day: cold, sugary black pudding swimming in a sauce composed of pig's blood and cranberries!

3

THE ARTS AND LETTERS

IN A PAINTER'S STUDIO

From an early age I lived among painters and painting. This was through no decision of my own, but the fact that I did so no doubt explains my precocious but lasting interest in colours and the world of colours. Three of my mother's uncles were painters and, even if I only knew one of them, Raymond, on my mother's side of the family all my great-aunts, uncles and aunts, cousins and even my great-grandmother, who died aged 96, lived in apartments that were full of paintings, some of them very big ones. On my father's side, the painters belonged not to the family but to his circle of close friends. They were all artists who identified more or less closely with the Surrealist movement and they all tried to live, more or less successfully, from their painting.

The painter Marcel Jean (1900–93) was older than my father but had been a friend of his for years. He had a studio at the bottom of Montmartre, in rue Hégésippe-Moreau, close to the Montmartre cemetery. On Sundays, my father would often take me there early in the morning, before going back up the rue Lepic to do the shopping. For me, those visits were real treats: this painter's studio, in a street with such an over-the-top first name – Hégésippe! – was, to me, truly an Aladdin's cave, the more so since Marcel Jean worked with many different techniques: oils, gouache, water colours, pastels, charcoal and others too. One particularly fascinated me as it involved a number of large tubs: this was flotation. Powdered pigments were scattered on to the surface of the water and, before they had time to dissolve or sink to the bottom, the painter would slip a sheet of paper into the tub and collect the marks and traces of colours that deposited weird shapes on it, shapes considered to be very significant and that the artist touched up hardly at all. Onto these floated sheets of paper, my father would sometimes transcribe one of his short poems in verse or in prose. My sister Isabelle still has a fine flotation produced by Marcel Jean, the predominant greens and blues of which lend it a mysterious air and, as it happens, it was on this flotation that my father set the poem that I like best of all, a serious, gentle poem that ends with the fine eight-syllable phrase: 'Se souvenir d'avoir aimé' (Remembering that one has loved).

But Marcel Jean's most usual medium was oil-painting and his studio was full of dozens of more or less empty tubes of paint with which I was allowed to play or to paint. On the Sundays when he was feeling generous, which were not very frequent, he would even let me take home a few used tubes that were destined for the dustbin but that, for me, were the best of presents. They were a joy to look at and to touch rather than to put to true creative use, for these almost empty, dried-up tubes, hard or impossible to open, were, to me, no good for painting once I had returned home. Not only was it practically impossible to unscrew the stoppers, but I possessed neither the materials nor the skill and knowledge necessary for oil-painting. Nevertheless, I was proud to possess such a treasure, to classify the tubes according to their colours, to stroke their heavy, smooth, lead surfaces and above all to show them to my jealous playmates, in particular Christian, who owned only a box of coloured crayons (a large collection, to be sure: maybe as many as two dozen, which was a lot for those days) that could be used only for colouring, not for painting.

I was not yet 10 years old, but classifying colours was already a recurrent pleasure for me. Whether I was doing so in my mother's pharmacy or in Marcel Jean's studio, I had the idea that there was a secret chromatic order that adults had overturned and that it was up to me to rediscover it, or even re-establish it. In this task, my favourite back-up materials consisted of medicament boxes and tubes of paint. These were at once precious objects and marvellous toys. Over the years, it was while working in these two 'chromatic laboratories' (the pharmacy and the painter's studio) rather than in primary school or in my *lycée* that I progressively devised a number of personal principles concerning colours. They were not particularly original but I elaborated them early on and have never since felt any need or desire to question them, not even when, having become a historian, I realized that there are no universal chromatic truths and that, on the contrary, everything changed from one society and from one period to another.

Those few principles that were forged in my childhood but have stayed with me in my adult life, in my work as a researcher and even in my modest activities as a 'Sunday painter', may be summed up as follows:

1. Black and white are colours in their own right.
2. There are only six basic colours: black, white, red, blue, yellow, and green.
3. Then come five second-rank colours, sometimes wrongly called 'half-colours': grey, brown, pink, purple and orange.
4. All other colours are simply nuances or nuances of nuances.

A PAINTER CAUGHT BETWEEN TWO VOLUMES

I grew up among books. At an early age, I realized that the truth of beings and things was to be found not so much in the realities of daily life as in libraries. My father's contained about 15,000 volumes, quite a few of which were art books. Surrealist painting was, of course, widely represented, but he also had more general works that were more accessible to the child that I was. To be honest, I looked mostly at the photographs, the majority being black-and-white, that were contained in the heavy volumes positioned on the lowest shelves. Among the fine-art books devoted to painting there was one that I found particularly intriguing: *L'Histoire de la peinture française* (The History of French Painting), published by Louis Dimier (2nd edn, 1934). It was divided into two volumes of equal size, the first of which was sub-titled *Des origines au retour de Simon Vouet de Rome* (From its Origins down to the

Return of Simon Vouet from Rome). This sub-title both disconcerted me and made me wonder.

'To the return of Simon Vouet from Rome'. Such a strange formulation for a sub-title! What was it all about? Surely some absolutely exceptional happening. Who could he be, this Simon Vouet, who had paid a visit to Rome at the time of the Three Musketeers and whose return to Paris had so radically changed the whole of French painting? What did he bring back with him? Unknown pigments? Splendid Italian reds? Incomparable greens? Blues from beyond the seas? For me, painting was – and still is – first and foremost a matter of colour. Of course, I knew nothing at all about Simon Vouet or his paintings. That was why I was so amazed that he should be considered the greatest of all French painters, the one whose return from Rome had divided the history of French painting into two volumes. He certainly must have been a genius: perhaps the French Raphael or Vermeer, two painters that I did know of and whom I had classed among the greatest. Curiously enough, this book's illustrations, relatively abundant but solely black-and-white, did not offer the reader any paintings by Vouet, either in the first volume or in the second; and what I could understand of the text was uninformative. What on earth could be the meaning of expressions such as 'the Baroque adapted to the Gallic genius' or 'the most illusionist of Roman French painters'?

The mystery remained unresolved until I was grown up. As an adolescent, my taste in painting veered away from the French seventeenth century. I preferred the Middle Ages and I was fascinated by illuminations. Thanks to my Aunt Lise, a Curator of Manuscripts in the Bibliothèque nationale, illuminated manuscripts had won me over and steered me away from the modern and contemporary paintings beloved by my father. I could not muster the curiosity to learn more about the enigmatic Simon Vouet (1590–1649).

Later, as a student and at the age when one is curious about everything and delights in consulting the reference books of large libraries for no good reason, I discovered by chance that Vouet had spent ten years in Rome, where he had become 'the most Italian of the French painters'. In 1627, Louis XIII, who subsidized him, recalled him to Paris and Vouet obediently returned. He brought with him not new pigments or unknown colours but artistic theories elaborated by the

Italian Baroque School. He set up a much-frequented studio, was the teacher of Eustache Le Sueur and Charles Le Brun and became an official court painter and, later, toward the end of his life, the rival of Poussin. Simon Vouet did not introduce a fashion for any particularly Roman red or any incomparable green or any blue from overseas. His painting palette differed little from that of other painters of his day. I was disappointed.

IN DARKENED HALLS

The first film that I saw in a cinema was *Twenty Thousand Leagues Beneath the Sea*, directed by Richard Fleischer, in which the principal roles were played by Kirk Douglas, James Mason and Peter Lorre. This was in 1954 and I was not yet 7. The film was in technicolour, which was fairly unusual in that period. According to the film-buffs it remains one of the best adaptations of Jules Verne to the cinema screen. Sadly, I have never seen it again.

Despite that first experience, which inevitably left its mark, for me cinema remains a black-and-white art. This makes me typical of my generation: a 'real' film is a film in black-and-white, and the history of the cinema is essentially a history in black-and-white. Sometimes I feel that colour has distorted the seventh art, which is no doubt why all my favourite films are black-and-white. Top of the list is Kenji Mizoguchi's *Tales of a Pale Moon after the Rain* (1953), which I reckon to be the best film ever made. In it, the crossing of Lake Biwa, at night, with the water shining, reflections of the moon, the slap of the oars and the distant echo of drums is, in my eyes, the most admirable scene in the whole history of the cinema. Next come Ingmar Bergman's *Midsummer Night* (1953) and *The Seventh Seal* (1957); *La Règle du jeu* (The Rules of the Game) (1939) by Jean Renoir; *The Night of the Hunter* (1955) by Charles Laughton; *8½* (1963) and *Amarcord* (1973) by Federico Fellini. There is nothing original about this list: its films head all the classificatory honours lists. I am a very ordinary film-goer.

My research into the history of colours nevertheless did lead me to take an interest in the beginning of cinema and showed me that, as in the case of photography, the transition from black-and-white to colour had involved plenty of difficulties and considerable resistance, not so much technical as, rather, of a social and moral nature. The first public showing (with a charge for admission) of the Cinematograph of the Lumière brothers took place in Paris, at the Grand Café on the Boulevard des Capucines, on 28 December 1895. As early as the following year, and for three decades thereafter, active research was undertaken with the aim of, for the first time, providing films with colour. Some experiments were fruitful but made little impact on commercial cinema. The animated images offered to the general public for a long time remained black-and-white ones.

The technical difficulties involved in producing films in colour were, it is true, immense. Initially, the film was hand-painted, using stencils, one for each colour, cut from the positive films. The colours were applied with a paintbrush and the toil was lengthy and detailed, impossible to use for a full-length film that included sets, costumes and make-up, all created using a range of greys. Then, for a while, films were tinged with colour by plunging them into baths of liquid dyed with colouring agents. This did create atmosphere and even atmospheric codes, as the same colouring agents were always chosen for scenes of the same type (blue for night-time, green for outdoor scenes, red for danger, yellow for joy); but it was still not cinema in colour. Later, coloured filters came to be used: first, at the time of projection; later on, while the scenes were being shot. Finally, as in engraving and in still photography, three rolls of film of three different colours were superimposed on one another to obtain all other colours. The first animated cartoon in colour (one of Walt Disney's famous 'Silly Symphonies') was shown in public in 1932. But it was another three years before a real colour film came out; this was Rouben Mamoulian's *Becky Sharp*.

Actually, the technicolour process, which dominated the early years of colour-cinema, had been elaborated as early as 1915. It continued to be perfected right up to the mid-1930s and, before World War II, made it possible to shoot masterpieces such as Michael Curtis's *The Adventures of Robin Hood* (1938) and Victor Fleming's *Gone with the Wind* (1939). Technically, however, it would have been possible to produce and market colour-films much earlier. The diffusion of technicolour to the general public was delayed not so much for technical or even financial reasons as for moral considerations. Around 1915–20, for the Puritanical capitalists – all of them Protestants, both in Europe and in the United States – who at that time controlled the production of images, just as they controlled that of mass-produced objects, animated cartoons constituted a frivolity or even an indecency. To go even further and present the general public with animated images in colour would be positively obscene. Hence the delay of two decades between being ready technically and being projected on to the cinema screens for the first time.

After World War II, colour films were more widely diffused, but not until the early 1970s did they come to outnumber black-and-white films. At this time attempts were made, without much success, to avoid giving cinematographic images a 'picture-postcard look'. Many aesthetes and creative artists deplored the invasive presence of colour and its unrealistic character. In the cinema, as on television and in magazines, colour occupied an exaggerated and distorting place in comparison to that which it holds in natural vision or everyday life. However, the general public did not fall into line and refused to return to black-and-white (which, however, true film-buffs did continue to demand for certain categories of films). The recent practice of 'colourizing' old films produced – and conceived! – in black-and-white certainly reflects the general public's taste for colour, particularly in the United States. Since American television-watchers (and soon, no doubt, European ones too) refuse to watch old black-and-white films, the only thing to do is to 'colourize' them (the very word is abominable) so that they can be shown on television. This has been happening since the 1980s and 1990s and it has given rise to perfectly legitimate disputes, not only legal and ethical but also aesthetic and artistic.

Today, it costs more to shoot a film in black-and-white than to do so in colour (and the same applies to photography). Among those who are truly creative, a swing in the pendulum of taste, the modes and systems of which are not unusual, has brought about a definite reappraisal of black-and-white, leading to a sense that it is more beguiling, more atmospheric, altogether more 'cinematographic'. Among some old cinema-goers, a certain snobbishness even inclines them to refuse to go to see films in colour. Even if one cannot share their views, one has to recognize that cinema is historically and mythologically a black-and-white world. 'Colourizing' old films will never alter that fact.

IVANHOE

Although my favourite films are all black-and-white, the one that left
its mark on me most strongly and played a decisive role in my youthful years was a colour film: Richard Thorpe's *Ivanhoe*, shot in 1952,
starring Robert Taylor, Elizabeth Taylor (still very young and breath-
takingly beautiful), Joan Fontaine and George Sanders. The film was
released on European screens in the following year, but I did not get
to see it until two years later. I was 8 years old and it was summer. In a
small town in Brittany, situated not far from the seaside resort where I
spent my holidays every year, the grandmother of one of my playmates
helped to run the parish cinema: one of modest means, in a rudimentary hall and with a noisy and temperamental projector that showed
third-rate copies of films. My friend and I sometimes acted as 'ush-
erettes', not to show people to their seats but to sell them sweets and
Esquimaux ice-creams. It was a chance for us to guzzle (in those days
all cinemas sold choc-ices) and also to see films for free, sometimes on
several afternoons or evenings in succession. In that July of 1955, for
one whole week I was able to watch Richard Thorpe's *Ivanhoe*, in the
French version. I saw it right through five or even six times. I remember
every sequence, every scene, every detail, every dialogue. The French
dialogue was unusually good; I would love to trace its authors and offer
them the congratulations that are their due.

Historians of the cinema have, however, not expressed much admiration for the *Ivanhoe* film and even less for Richard Thorpe, whom a
number of critics described as 'a laborious film-maker': a most unjust
judgement. *Ivanhoe* is a magnificent adventure story, of the kind that
Hollywood produced in the early 1950s. The attack on the castle of
Torquilstone and the final ordeal are two great moments of cinema.
And, on general release, the film has enjoyed an exceptional international career. Furthermore, as a historian of the Middle Ages, I consider *Ivanhoe* to be one of the best films made about this period. The
landscapes, castles, costumes, armour, décors and general atmosphere
are all essentially faithful to historical reality, or at least to our image
of that reality. The action takes place at the end of the twelfth century
and, for the first and possibly only time in cinema, the knights have
the arms and coats of arms of the late twelfth century, not those of the

fifteenth or sixteenth century. Thanks to this fidelity, the film plunges its spectators into a universe at once familiar and fabulous. I deplore the fact that studies of the American cinema are so scornful of it, all the more given that it prompted my fascination with the Middle Ages, with banners, shields and the interplay of their colours. At the age of 8, I as yet knew nothing about heraldry, but the escutcheons of the hero's two main enemies already impressed me: Hugh de Bracy's *gueules à la fasce d'or* (gules with golden fesse) and Brian de Bois-Guilbert's *bandé et contre-bandé d'azur et d'argent* (bended and counter-bended with azure and argent). What could be more simple, more direct, more graphic? From that summer of 1955 onward, I definitely preferred knights to cowboys.

The following summer, in that same local cinema in Brittany, I saw *The Knights of the Round Table*, also directed by Richard Thorpe, but I was less enchanted by it. Despite the presence of Ava Gardner – Ava Gardner! – it was less successful than *Ivanhoe*, less bracing and, to be honest, rather kitsch. To adapt Arthurian legend to the cinema is an impossible task: one only has to think of Robert Bresson's *Lancelot du Lac* (1974), a disastrous film, or John Boorman's monstrous *Excalibur* (1981), so noisily grotesque as to leave one aghast. That legend is too ineffable for the cinema screen.

Of course, *Ivanhoe* was easier to film, for Walter Scott's novel provided everything: the scenario, the historical figures, the characters, the places, the settings, the costumes, the colours and the medieval arms. Walter Scott had imagined everything, described everything, foreseen everything right down to the continuity editing of the major scenes: the return from the crusade, the tournament, the attack on the castle, the trial for witchcraft and the judgement of God.

When his book appeared in December 1891, Scott was 48 years old. He had been a famous writer for several years, in Scotland as well as England. But with *Ivanhoe* he was more ambitious than with his earlier novels. The story unfolds in the heart of the Middle Ages, entirely in England, during the absence of King Richard the Lionheart, who had gone off on a crusade and been taken prisoner on the return journey. While he was held in captivity, first in Austria, then in Germany, his brother, Prince John, tried to seize power, supported by the Norman barons in his struggle against the last of the Saxon lords, who had remained loyal to Richard. Into this setting of a divided England await-ing the return of its king, the author introduced a number of other dramatic storylines: the conflict between an authoritarian father and a son thirsty for freedom, the impossible love between a Jewish girl and the Christian hero, the secret identity of a mysterious 'black knight'. These were interwoven with the various spectacular events mentioned above.

The book enjoyed a considerable and immediate success and brought Walter Scott fame and fortune. The Universities of Oxford and Cambridge each offered him an honorary doctorate; Scottish intel-lectual society showered him with honours and even invited him to preside over the prestigious Royal Society of Edinburgh; and, finally, the new king, George IV, granted him a title of nobility, making him a baronet. All these honours came his way in the six months following the appearance of his book. The year 1820 was certainly the most glorious of Walter Scott's life and he owed it all to *Ivanhoe*. His celebrity also brought him wealth. Between that date and his death (1832), his book sold over a million and a half copies in various editions and translations. It was a gold-mine! Unfortunately, though, it dried up, owing to badly judged investments in imprudent editorial ventures, followed by bank-ruptcy (in 1826) and huge debts that took the writer six years to pay off, destroying both his art and his health. Scott was a talented writer but a disastrous businessman.

In an enquiry conducted in 1983–4 by the French journal *Mediévales*, targeting young researchers and committed historians, one of the ques-tions asked was: 'Where did you get your taste for the Middle Ages?' One-third of the people who responded declared that they owed their precocious vocation to *Ivanhoe*, either in its form as a book, usually a special version for adolescents, or else in Richard Thorpe's version of the story, which they had seen in the cinema. So my own case was by no means exceptional: numerous medievalists owed their first attrac-tion to the Middle Ages, and subsequently their vocation, to *Ivanhoe*, a book and film in which colours play a role of the first importance. When we imagine the Middle Ages, we associate them primarily with colours.

'VOWELS'

You must forgive me: I do not like Rimbaud – neither the man nor his oeuvre. I have never really understood what was admirable about being a rebellious young poet. It is a fairly common condition and was possibly even more so in 1870 than it is today. As for Rimbaud's poetry, I confess that it does not move me. I find it jerky, artificial, with neither the airy musicality of Verlaine nor the bewitching strangeness of Nerval. I hope that admirers of Rimbaud – I know there are very many of them – will not hold it too much against me. My rejection of this poet is probably due to an anti-father revolt: my father's love for Rimbaud was boundless and he had collected an incomparable library of his works. Unfortunately I, in my stubbornness, never went near it until I reached adulthood. It was thus in a school text-book that I discovered the famous sonnet, 'Vowels', which I proceeded to learn and comment upon. In those days this was a compulsory task for any student in the top literature class. I well remember the enthusiasm of our teacher, who tried to get us to share his emotion, as he commented on the relations between colours and syllables, and colours and music, citing as an example the famous ocular harpsichord of Father Castel (around 1735–40) in which sounds were replaced by colours, then drawing our attention to Baudelaire's *Correspondences* and to the synaes-thesia of Proust. He was successful in capturing our attention and an argument ensued to discover who, in the class, associated with the five vowels the same colours as Rimbaud did.

> A noir, E blanc, I rouge, U vert, O bleu: voyelles,
> Je dirai quelque jour vos naissances latentes . . .
> (A black, E white, I red, U green, O blue: vowels,
> I shall one day sing of your latent births . . .)

The class consisted of around thirty-five pupils, all of them boys; and not one said that he shared the associations suggested in the first line of the sonnet. Not one. It is true that some did not react at all or divulge their own alphabet of colours (in the mid-sixties, in literature lessons, even if rowdy pupils were rare, somnolent ones were not). But for several of us it was 'clear' that A could not be black, nor could E be white. And as for associating I with the colour red . . . One of my class-mates, bolder than the rest of us (I remember only that his first name was Pierre), was courageous enough to suggest that Arthur Rimbaud had deliberately written a poem about associations that ran contrary to good sense and general perceptions. It was a sensible remark but it did not please our teacher at all. He kept on repeating, 'But you must read the sonnet right to the end!'

He was quite right. But that first line, written in an exclamatory mode, was much too overwhelming; it crushed the next thirteen lines and, on its own, constituted a chromatic palette, colour-range and hori-zon so strong that it seemed to make it unnecessary to read the lines that followed. Anyway, I am not certain that reading the poem right through does throw much light on the suggested list. After all, one of the properties of poetry is precisely that it never does deliver up all its mysteries.

Rimbaud, who was frequently asked about the meaning of the sonnet and his distribution of colours among the vowels, always declared that his choices were 'arbitrary and gratuitous', which is why some inter-preters have regarded the poem simply as a kind of hoax. Others, far more numerous, have produced many glosses and meta-glosses in an attempt to seize upon the poem's meaning and explain this alphabet of colours, referring to primary ones and complementary ones and warm ones and cold ones, underlining on the one hand the opposition between black and white and, on the other, the spectrum, and won-dering about the 'shapes' of the letters, the 'feet' of the A, the three crossbars of the E, the verticality of the I, all of them shapes that may be related to objects or living beings that are the same colours as those proposed in the poem. An ocean of bibliographies has been devoted to this sonnet, causing Tristan Tzara to exclaim ironically, 'Vowels, vowels, what a fuss you have stirred up!'

Perhaps that was indeed the poet's more or less conscious pur-pose. Rimbaud was 17 years old when he composed his sonnet in late summer, 1871. He had just completed his obscure 'Bateau ivre' (The Drunken Ship), which he was to recite at a dinner given by the Parisian literary group known as 'Les vilains Bonhommes' (The Ugly Fellows). At that date he had not yet visited England (that was to be in the fol-lowing year), but he was already going through 'an English phase' and liked to play about with vocabulary of the language that he had learned in school, in Charleville. Quite possibly, the vowel sonnet originated from a simple schoolboy pun on Rimbaud/rainbow.

I still remember the choices that I myself made at the time of this textual analysis attempted, in 1964, in my *lycée*. Like Rimbaud, I was almost 17 and, like him, I would have been hard put to it to explain my choices. But the sequence that immediately came to mind was one that I would not reject even today: A red, E blue, I yellow, O white, U blue or green. In my coloured alphabet there was no black. I cannot quite recall the choices made by my classmates, but I do remember that, for practically the whole class, A was red. That choice was virtually unanimous. Since then, I have sometimes asked friends to participate in this Rimbaudian exercise in vowels. The palettes proposed were naturally not all identical but a majority of participants always associated A with red, and slightly fewer of them associated U with blue.

Is it possible to experiment in this way with consonants? Their music is different and the sonorous colours are harder to identify. However, I think I would be inclined to classify F and T within a range of whites, H and M as reds, J and N as yellows and only Z would be completely black. Because of candied liquorice or because of Zorro?

THE RED AND THE BLACK

I do not like Rimbaud, nor do I relish Stendhal. I must be a kind of literary barbarian. But my admiration for Flaubert is so great that I find it hard to appreciate Stendhal. How can one bear to read or reread *Le Rouge et le Noir* when one has read *L'Éducation sentimentale*? How can one avoid comparing these two novelists one generation apart? I read *Le Rouge et le Noir* when still quite young, no doubt too young, around the age of 16, on the advice of my literature teacher. Later, I read it again, when I was over 40; but in the meantime I had devoured the whole of Flaubert . . .

Stendhal's novel seems to me crushed by its title, a magnificent one which, however, captures the reader's attention too much, leading him down paths of symbolism that may not have been those envisaged by the author. Anyway, what did Stendhal mean when he chose that title? We do not know, for he never explained why he chose those two colours. All we know is that initially the novel was entitled *Julien*, after the name of its hero Julien Sorel, and that the author opted instead for *Le Rouge et le Noir* in May 1830, a few months before its definitive publication.

Stendhal's silence has engendered a considerable bibliography. Every critic of the work proposed his own interpretation and his own hypotheses. Many have seen Red as the colour of the army and Black as that of the Church. The title could thus be considered to evoke the uncertainty of the hero: should he be a soldier or a priest, should he follow a military career or an ecclesiastical one? This explanation, which is widely accepted, is undermined by the conjunction that links the two colour-terms. What Stendhal wrote was not 'Le Rouge ou le Noir', but 'Le Rouge et le Noir'. A more simplistic explanation sees in the red Julien's crime and in the black his death on the scaffold. But some critics switch the meaning of the colours round: the black stands for sin, the red for the executioner. Around 1830, the expression 'mourir avec le collet rouge' (to die with a red collar) meant 'to die beheaded'.

Another, more fragile trail led in the direction of red being the colour of Madame de Rênal and black being that of Mathilde de la Mole, the two women who loved Julien. But in truth not many elements in the novel support such a theory. In contrast, a number of scholars have seen the two colours as those of a pack of playing cards or those used for gambling in a casino. One even ran to ground a game of chance called 'red and black', an ancestor of the twentieth century's game of *trente et quarante*. Here, the idea is that the title of the novel underlines the way in which Julien's destiny is played out by chance, for he entrusts it to the whims of Fortune. Yet others carried the symbolism even further, suggesting that the novel's title refers to Julien Sorel's astral influences: red, the colour of brutal passion and jealousy is associated with the planet Mars; black, the colour of twisted ambitions and warped souls, is associated with Saturn. Why not? In the 1820s, colour symbolism was fashionable and led interpretations of it deep into the specious twists and turns of astrology and the esoteric. But was all this not going a bit too far?

Literary historians know that, in the period when Stendhal was writing his masterpiece, there were many novels, especially in England, whose titles used the names of colours. When his choice alighted upon *Le Rouge et le Noir*, Henri Beyle was not being at all original and was running a risk of which he was perhaps unaware: colour-terms are strong terms, very strong ones and they always suggest more than one intends them to. They cannot be used with impunity.

CHRÉTIEN DE TROYES AT THE CINEMA

Only twice have I acted as a historical adviser for a film set in the Middle Ages. Both occasions were instructive experiences, not so much on account of what they taught me about the other side of the camera, a world then unknown to me, but because of the questions put to me by the film director, questions that historians practically never did ask themselves: how did people greet one another in the twelfth or four-teenth century? What gestures did they make? How did they sit down to table? At which moments of the day did monks wear their cowls and at which did they go bare-headed (a matter that was of budgeting inter-est when working out how many of the actors needed tonsures . . .)?

My first experience was very low-key. The film was Eric Rohmer's *Perceval*, released in February 1979. A few years previously I had pub-lished, with Hachette, a work entitled *La Vie quotidienne au temps des chevaliers de la Table Ronde* (Daily life at the time of the knights of the Round Table). It was my first book, written during my military service in the deserted library of the Musée de l'Armée. Rohmer wished to consult me about costumes, coats of arms and colours. On two con-secutive days, he came to consult me in my office at the Bibliothèque nationale, in the department of medals, where I worked as a young curator. This was at the end of the month of January 1978, and they were extremely cold days made worse by the central-heating breaking down. Rohmer seemed oblivious of this. He stayed for a long time, put many questions to me, took many notes and invited me to lunch in a Chinese restaurant. I was shy, partly because he too seemed to be, with a timidity that is always intimidating to others. We talked at length about the coats of arms of the knights of the Round Table, and even longer about the colours of clothing and sets. Several examples of coats of arms were chosen, once I had described them using the technical terms of heraldry that so delighted Rohmer. Similarly, we decided upon the colours for the costumes to be worn by the principal protagonists: green for Percival, blue for Gawain, white for Arthur, black for Keu, red for the Red Knight and yellow for Gornemant de Goort. That was the full extent of my collaboration.

One year later, when I saw the film at a preview in a cinema in Montparnasse, I was most surprised. Rohmer had paid not the slightest attention to the choices we had made about what to use and what to reject. The escutcheons were not heraldic; the costumes were unlike those that we had designed together, and bore very little relation to those of the twelfth century; the colouring of the sets was kitsch to varying degrees. I remembered, for instance, that one year earlier I had told Rohmer, 'Above all, no purple; the colour did not exist at the time of Chrétien de Troyes; it is sham medieval, not the real thing'. But in the film, purple was everywhere. I never dared to ask the great director the reasons for these differences and mistakes. Had he lost his notes? Had he placed more trust in his team of stage designers than in the youthful historian that I then was? Or had he deliberately distanced himself from a particular reality, preferring in this respect, as throughout the film, a poetic distancing rather than a meticulous historical and literary reconstruction? I shall never know.

PINK PIGS AND BLACK PIGS

My second collaboration with a film director took place several years later, in 1984–5. I belonged to a group of historians gathered round Jacques Le Goff to act as advisers to Jean-Jacques Annaud, who was preparing to film *The Name of the Rose*, based on Umberto Eco's novel of the same name. I was responsible, in particular, for matters of colour, emblems and monastic clothing. Annaud's plan was different from Rohmer's. He was aiming for a recreation of the places, costumes and material life of the early fourteenth century that was as faithful as possible, hoping that such a recreation, based on the recent research of historians and archaeologists, would transport spectators into another world, acting as a discovery or even an education. What was expected of us, before the film crew began shooting, was to collect as much documentation as possible and then, in collaboration with the set and costume designers and the stage managers and their team, to make the correct choices for every scene and every character. The whole undertaking was an enormous machine, backed up by a considerable budget and collaborators of every kind. It was not easy to do a good job in an operation so compartmentalized and subject to so many stages of approval, many of them contradictory: so much to-ing and fro-ing between the various teams and decision-takers in order to settle upon the cut of a costume, its colour, its insignia and its accessories! Several times I was tempted to give it all up. Furthermore, Umberto Eco, who was a friend of Jacques Le Goff, would sometimes join our little group and, when he did so, work became out of the question: his polyglot humour, his burlesque and subversive loquaciousness and his gleeful anecdotes ruled out all serious activity.

All the same, we did complete our part of the work on time. However, when, in our absence, the shooting of the film had already begun and a scene involving a herd of pigs was about to be filmed, I realized that I had forgotten to tell Jean-Jacques Annaud's collaborators that, in the fourteenth century, pigs were neither pink nor white, but usually black, grey, brown or spotted. They looked more like wild boars than modern pigs. As a specialist in colours and animals and hired on those grounds, I was not proud of myself. Shamefaced, I found the courage to alert Jacques Le Goff, who warned Jean-Jacques Annaud. But time was pressing. It would be hard to lay hands on black pigs and transport them to the place in Italy where the film was being shot, and doing so was likely to add further delays to those already incurred. What was to be done? With permission from the director, one of the stage-managers came to a hasty decision: they would make do with the few black pigs that were already available, and the hides of the rest, which were of an extremely modern pink, would be sprayed with black paint. This operation went ahead. I learned later that the paint had been of poor quality, that the pigs had rubbed up against one another, got dirty and rolled in the mud. Their appearance took on a blotchy look and the whole scene, which was anyway expected to be rather mucky, became, according to the technicians, 'filthy and bestial'. Jean-Jacques Annaud, who was keen to emphasize the uncouth nature of fourteenth-century peasant life, was apparently well satisfied.

Historically, it was apparently in the second half of the eighteenth century that European pigs began to display really pale coats, verging on white or pink, instead of their former grey, black, reddish or spotted ones of the past. The reasons for this paler look were explained by more drastic procedures for selecting particular species in order to produce more and better-quality meat, and by crossing English sows with stud-boars imported from South-East Asia. These Asiatic porkers had paler coats, like the strange 'Siamese pig' whose snub nose had so fascinated Buffon. Such cross-breeding operations, and others too, progressively generated new races of pigs, such as the renowned Berkshire pig – an animal which, at but 2 years of age, might weigh over 400 kilos – and, later on, the famous white-skinned 'Large White', which is still the dominant species in European livestock. Both are animals that are rarely seen on our screens.

WHEN DALÍ ASSIGNED MARKS

I never met Salvador Dalí, but my father used to spend time with him in the pre-war years and was often invited to his house in the 14th *arrondissement*, not far from the Montsouris park. Actually, he was closer to Gala and it was she whom he really visited. According to him, 'little Dalí' spent most of the day sleeping and had his assistants paint the major portion of his paintings, to which he would then add a few finishing touches. How true was that? My father, who never invented untruths, did sometimes exaggerate. He was friendly with Eluard, was distressed by his separation from Gala and regarded Dalí more or less as an intruder or even an imposter. However, he was fascinated by Gala and would sometimes accompany her to the Saint-Ouen flea-market where, he told me, she would look in particular for pieces of material or clothes in bright colours. She showed a marked preference for red and purple.

As for myself, although I have never been a great admirer of Dalí's painting, several of his books have intrigued and fascinated me. One was the juicy *50 Secrets magiques pour peindre* (50 magic secrets for painting), published first in 1948 in New York, then, three years later, in Paris. It is a kind of treatise in which Dalí recounts experiences, records a number of recipes – most of them somewhat enigmatic, if not surreal – and, more seriously, presents an analysis of the various qualities required in order to be a painter. This leads him to distinguish nine parameters and to compare the strengths of eleven great artists. The nine parameters listed are: technique, inspiration, colour, subject matter, genius, composition, originality, mystery and authenticity; the masters are Leonardo, Raphael, Velásquez, Vermeer, Ingres, Manet, Meissonier, Bouguereau, Mondrian, Picasso and Dalí himself. In an extraordinary comparative table, each painter is given a mark (out of 20), evaluating his merit or talent with respect to each of the nine qualities.

The result is gleeful and, knowing Dalí, this comes as no surprise. Mondrian's role is that of a foil: throughout, he obtains a mark equal to 0, except for originality (0.5), composition (1) and authenticity (3). Meissonier and Bouguereau fare no better, obtaining lamentable marks, except for authenticity (respectively, 18 and 15) and, for Meissonier, for mystery (17). Manet is treated equally harshly, which is more surprising, receiving no mark higher than 6, except for authenticity (14). On the other hand, Dalí's admiration for the great masters of the past is reflected in the astronomical marks that he gives them: Leonardo and Velásquez score nothing below 15; Raphael nothing below 18; as for Vermeer, he scores 20 throughout, except for a 19 for originality. According to this astonishing collection of marks, Vermeer is the greatest painter of all time.

A trio of painters stands out clearly from the rest: Vermeer, Raphael and Velásquez. Leonardo comes in fourth place, throughout receiving slightly lower marks than those of the three others – Raphael, in particular. As Dalí sees it, the judgement passed in the lifetimes of the two painters – which placed Raphael higher than Leonardo – was legitimate, even if the verdict of posterity has been otherwise. However, the most remarkable and most delectable judgement is not to be found here, but in the compared marks of Dalí and Picasso. Not only does Dalí give himself marks but, above all, he marks his friend, compatriot and rival, Picasso. One may even suspect that, for Dalí, this is the essential point of this whole comparative table and that the nine other painters, including the geniuses of the past, are only there to dress up the Dalí versus Picasso 'match'.

Of course, the victor in this match is Dalí himself: he receives no lower-than-average marks and three sumptuous 19s out of 20, in authenticity, genius and, above all, mystery – whereas Picasso receives, respectively, 7, 20 and 2. Picasso is not a painter of 'mystery'! Nevertheless, he does come out ahead of Dalí three times, but only just: in genius (20 as opposed to 19), in inspiration (19 as opposed to 17) and in subject matter (19 as opposed to 18). But, for the other six parameters, it is Dalí who wins – and does so hands down, in some cases. The worst mark received by Picasso is without question a lamentable 2 out of 20, in mystery (for which Dalí gives himself 19!), but his most unexpected mark – and the most subtle and delicious in this whole marksheet – is a modest 7 out of 20 in originality. Here Dalí reveals all his finesse, all his malice, all his jealousy: not 1 out of 20, or 18 or 19 – no: a miserable and memorable 7 out of 20. As Dalí sees it, this puts Picasso in his place.

It is worth noting, finally, that where the colour parameter alone is concerned, the worst painters are Mondrian and Meissonier (0 out of 20), and the best is Vermeer (20 out of 20). Here Dalí awards himself the average mark of 10 out of 20 and gives Picasso 9 out of 20, which, simply where colour is concerned, is all-in-all quite generous to Picasso, a mediocre colourist, as Pablo himself willingly recognized.

THE COLOURS OF A GREAT PAINTER

For Dalí, Vermeer is the greatest of all painters – as he is for me, even though I know full well that to award such an accolade makes very little sense and that to compare artists who are incomparable is a somewhat futile, even scandalous, exercise. But very early on, at the age of 15 or 16, I discovered that Vermeer was my favourite painter. In the years that followed, I have never changed that early opinion. Of all his works, the one that I liked best was, right from the start, *The Alleyway* (Amsterdam, Rijksmuseum), not the more famous *View of Delft* or *The Girl Wearing a Turban* (The Hague, Mauritzhuis). That preference is in no way original. For it is shared by many artists and art critics. As early as 1884, for example, the German painter Max Liebermann, on his return from a visit to the Netherlands, wrote that *The Alleyway* was the finest of all easel paintings. I agree with him.

It is to my father that I owe a habit that I have followed throughout my life: visiting museums and art exhibitions. In the course of fifty years, I have visited a large number of them. Many provided me with an opportunity to make discoveries and experience revelations, others set off veritable infatuations that lasted for several years, but the exhibition that definitely enchanted me the most was the Johannes Vermeer show put on in the Mauritzhuis Museum in the Hague from March to June 1996. It was very popular, but I was lucky enough to visit it in excellent conditions one April evening, at twilight, with my friend Claudia, who shares my love of paintings. At a time when people from all over the world were flocking to see the collection of twenty-seven paintings attributed to an artist whose preserved works are few in number, on that evening, miraculously, there were no crowds. The pokiness of the exhibition rooms which, as a rule, constitutes a real discomfort, instead lent the visit an intimate air that was perfectly in keeping with the works exhibited. Among them was *The Alleyway*, which I had already admired on several occasions in the Amsterdam Rijksmuseum, but which I never tired of contemplating again and again.

The exhibition itself incorporated an annexe that presented the results of the most recent laboratory analyses carried out in order to gain a better understanding of the techniques and materials employed by Vermeer. The analyses were very scholarly, but the main conclusions of the chemists and physicists who had studied the works of the painter from Delft were set out in an accessible manner: neither Vermeer's pigments nor his binding agents, nor even the techniques that he adopted, were any different from those of other painters of his day. This was a cheering result, for it confirmed that Vermeer's genius lay elsewhere.

Outside a laboratory, that is to say at a museum or an exhibition, it is hard fully to appreciate the palette of a painter from the past. This is not only because we see the colours that he applied to the canvas or panel as they have weathered with the passing of time and not in their original state, but also because we see them in lighting conditions very different from those familiar to the artist and his period (these are essential matters to which I shall be returning). Having said that, though, it is less difficult to study the palette of a seventeenth-century painter than that of an eighteenth-century one. In the age of the Enlightenment, many novelties were introduced in the domain of pigments, and the old recipes for choosing, grinding, mixing and applying colours were upset and in competition with new practices that varied from one artist's studio to another. Furthermore, Newton's discoveries and the general recognition of the spectrum at the end of the previous century progressively altered the order of colours: red was no longer half way between white and black; green was now definitely thought of as a mixture of blue and yellow; and notions of primary colours and complementary ones gradually became established, as did ideas of warm colours and cold colours (in the sense that we understand today). By the end of the eighteenth century, the world of colours was not at all as it had been at its beginning.

In the period between 1655 and 1675, when Vermeer was active, the scene was quite different. Seventeenth-century innovations in the domain of pigments were few and far between. The only important novelty was the use of 'Naples yellow', which up until then had been reserved for ceramics. Contrary to the assertions made by some writers before the analyses of 1994–6, Vermeer appears to have been extremely classical in the pigments that he used. His originality and genius should be sought not in the materials that he employed, but in the way that he made light speak. His pigments were those of his age. For his blues, often very bright, he used lapis lazuli. But as this pigment was extremely costly, it was reserved for surface work; beneath it, the first layer came from azurite or smalt (used in particular for skies). For yellows, apart from the ochre bases, which had been used since very ancient times, there was plenty of yellow derived from tin and a certain amount of the new 'Naples yellow' from Italy (a lead antimoniate), but this was less common. As for greens, those derived from copper, which were unstable and corrosive, were little used, but many varieties of green bases were popular with most seventeenth-century painters. In this period, it was still unusual for artists to mix yellow and blue pigments in order to obtain green. Some did, of course, but it was above all in the following century that – to the great displeasure of some painting moralists – this practice became common. Finally, reds were obtained from vermilion, minium, cochenille or madder lacquer, woods from Brazil and red ochre in various shades.

Such was the palette of Vermeer brought to light by the laboratory analyses: nothing very original about it and it comprised in total fewer than twenty or so pigments. But as soon as one moves on from the palette of pigments to concentrate on the optical palette – which is, of course, essentially what counts – Vermeer is nothing like his contemporaries. The colouring in his painting is more harmonious, smoother, more delicate. This is due to his incomparable efforts to make the light active. His work depends on velvety notes and minute finishing touches and is based on the use of warm under-layers topped by cold, translucent tints. Historians of painting have said all or almost all there is to say about this aspect of Vermeer's talent. Few, however, have really had much to say about the colours themselves.

This is not the place to go into details, but I must underline the role played by the greys, especially the light greys: it is often upon them that the whole chromatic economy of the picture rests. Next, I must emphasize the quality of the blues. Vermeer is a painter of blue (and even of blue and white, for these two colours operate together in his paintings). It is perhaps his work with blues that distinguishes him from the other seventeenth-century Dutch painters: whatever their talent and their qualities, they do not know how to play upon blues with such subtlety. Finally – following Marcel Proust – we must still, and always, remember, in Vermeer's paintings, the importance of the little areas of yellow, some of them slightly pinkish (such as the famous 'little patch of yellow wall' in *A view of Delft*), others more acid. These yellows, sometimes hardly noticeable, seem to underpin all the musicality of Vermeer that enchants us so much and makes him a painter like no other.

HISTORIANS WITHOUT COLOURS

As a young, enthusiastic and naive researcher, in the mid-seventies I began to be interested in the history of colours and all its problems. My family environment, acquaintanceship with painters, regular visits to museums, pathological sensitivity to the colours of clothing and a recent thesis on medieval heraldry that I had submitted had all prepared me and steered me toward such research studies. I thought they would be easy and well worthwhile, welcomed in historian circles and already undertaken by numerous researchers. I could not have been more mistaken. At that time, among historians, archaeologists and art-historians, nobody, absolutely nobody, showed the slightest interest in colours. Even in fields in which it was reasonable to suppose one would discover ongoing studies on such a subject, colour was conspicuous by its absence. The history of clothing, for example, was a totally colourless history. Although documentation existed, masses of it, even for ancient periods, costume specialists were not interested. All that mattered were the archaeology of shapes and the nature of the various garments that had made up clothing over the years. The idea of a 'clothing system', lodged at the heart of social life and within which colours might have played an essential role, was completely foreign to them. As was the name of Roland Barthes . . .

But there was worse to come: the history of painting. In this discipline in which colour should, by its very nature, have occupied a place of the first importance, it was almost always passed over in silence. Entire thick, scholarly volumes were written on the oeuvre of a particular painter or pictorial movement, in which the authors made no mention at all of colours: 300 or 500 pages without formulating a single idea, a single remark, a single word about colours, not even a mention of terms such as 'blue', 'red' or 'yellow': that was quite an achievement! But such practices were normal, almost general, in the mid-seventies. Colour was the great missing element in the history of art.

I came down to earth. But there were more discoveries in the offing. After a few months of enquiries and reflections on the history of colours – more or less virgin ground – I realized that my work was not well received. Either such a subject seemed lacking in *gravitas*, or even frivolous (despite the fact that I had started off with historiography), or else it seemed altogether pointless, at once useless and impossible to work on. Furthermore, it was considered more or less immoral. This was a time when historians – and, more generally, all researchers in the humanities – had duties toward society but very little in the way of rights, certainly not the right to enjoyment. The idea that the individual pleasure of a researcher could be the prime motive for his or her work was not in tune with the times or was positively condemned. It seemed that I was deriving too much pleasure from my enquiries into the history of colours. My attitude was individualistic, almost indecent or even dangerous and, in any case, contrary to the ethics of research.

I had encountered a similar hostility a few years earlier when embarking upon my thesis on the medieval heraldic bestiary, a subject that my supervisors and my friends alike considered ridiculous, given that it was based on a despised discipline – heraldry – and on a subject of study unworthy of scholarly history: namely, animals. In the 1960s, animals were still relegated to 'minor history', collections of anecdotes and *curiosa* intended to ridicule the knowledge, practices and beliefs of our ancestors. Only a handful of philologists and a few historians of religion had taken an interest in some specific dossier within whose confines animals could be mentioned; but the very notion of devoting a study or an actual university thesis to them was unthinkable, almost suicidal. Since those days the situation has, happily, changed, and animals have now become a subject for history in their own right.

That is not yet quite the case of colour, even though mind-sets have evolved and important research – for the most part collective – has been conducted in this field. Even today, in 2010, historians of painting – many of them colleagues or friends of mine – take no interest in anything to do with colour. Some of them even prefer to study the works of this or that painter of the sixteenth or seventeenth century using black-and-white photographs rather than colour reproductions. The idea in their heads is that colour upsets the way that we look at things, it cheats on documented reality, misleads a researcher and prevents him studying style properly. Style: in the history of painting that word is sacrosanct! In vain do I explain to these friends and colleagues that every painter has a colour style of his own and that this deserves to be studied just as drawing, lines and volumes do . . . but it is all to no avail.

No doubt these are the last reverberations from a controversy that for many years has set in opposition the partisans of drawing and those of colouring. Which is the more important in the plastic arts? Form or colour? Drawing or colouring? In Renaissance Italy, such arguments resurface frequently, as they did in earlier times. Certain artists were even then beginning to wonder about the status of colours in painting, and then about the comparative merits of drawing and colouring when it came to expressing the truth of beings and things. In Florence, where many painters were also architects and neo-Platonic themes invaded all forms of artistic creation, drawing was thought to be more exact, more precise, more 'true'; in Venice they believed the opposite. The argument now took off. It was to continue for two centuries, firing artists and philosophers with passion, first in Italy, then in France and elsewhere in Europe.

The opponents of colour were not short of arguments. They judged colouring to be less noble than drawing because, unlike the latter, it was a product not of the mind but only of pigments and matter. Drawing is a prolongation of an idea; it addresses the intellect. Colour, for its part, addresses only the senses. It does not aim to inform, only to be seductive. By so doing, it sometimes upsets the way one sees things, prevents one seeing contours and identifying figures properly. Its seduction is wrong, for it turns one away from the True and the Good. In short, it is nothing but a cosmetic, falsity, deception and betrayal – all ideas already developed by Saint Bernard in the twelfth century, taken up by the great Protestant reformers and set centre-stage between 1550 and 1700 by the partisans of *disegno* over *colorito*. These long-standing reproaches are sometimes extended by the notion that colour is dangerous because it is uncontrollable: it defies language (naming colours and their nuances is an uncertain exercise) and it eludes all generalization, if not all analysis. Colour is rebellious; one should beware of it.

Opposing this view, the partisans of colouring emphasize all that drawing on its own, without colour, fails to convey: not only the emotional dimension of painting but also, quite simply, distinctions between zones and planes, the hierarchy of figures, the interplay of echoes and correspondences. Colour is not just sensual or musical, it also plays a classificatory role, indispensable in the teaching of certain sciences (zoology, botany, cartography, medicine). However, for its fans, its superiority lies elsewhere: only colour can give life to beings of flesh and blood. Only colour is painting, for there can be no painting except of living beings (an influential idea that pervaded the Age of Enlightenment). One should imitate not Leonardo or Michelangelo, but the Venetian masters – above all Titian – for they are the painters who excelled in the depiction of flesh and its tints.

These were the ideas that seemed to triumph in the late seventeenth century and the early eighteenth. At this point colour was, furthermore, relieved of some of its unpredictable and dangerous characteristics, since science now knew how to measure it, control it and reproduce it at will. Newton's work opened up the path to new discoveries, new classifications and new issues. But the arguments were still not over. Between 1830 and 1860 they resurfaced, particularly in France: now it was Ingres versus Delacroix, the supporters of drawing against the supporters of colour. And so it went on.

Taking other forms, this 'match' went on right down to the twentieth century, not only between historians of art but also between artists
themselves. Yves Klein (1928–62), for example, on numerous occasions
vigorously defended the primacy of colour over drawing. He produced
a declaration with which I am happy to identify: 'For me, colours are
living beings . . ., the true inhabitants of space. A line, for its part,
merely journeys through space, travels across it. It just passes through.'

THE WORKINGS OF TIME

My first attempts to research into the history of colours soon made me
aware of just how arduous a task tackling such a subject would be. It
took no more than a few months for me to understand why I had no
predecessors: attempting to put together such a history was and still
is an almost impossible task. Historians of clothing and art-historians
have many legitimate excuses to justify their silence on the subject of
colour over long decades. The task is too difficult. Not only with regard
to the method to adopt and the questions to resolve, but also simply at
the level of documentation.

On the monuments, works of art, objects and images that past ages
have handed down to us, the colours that we see are not in their original
state but are what the passing of time has made them. In some cases,
the difference is considerable. But the workings of time – whether due
to chemical changes in the colouring agents or, as the centuries have
passed, to the intervention of human beings who have over-painted and
repainted, modified, cleaned, varnished or suppressed certain layers of
colour laid down by previous generations – in themselves constitute
historical documentation. So what is to be done? Should we employ
extremely sophisticated modern techniques in order to 'restore' the
colours, trying to recapture their original state? To do so would involve
an element of positivism that I regard as at once dangerous and also
contrary to the mission of the historian: the workings of time are
an integral part of his research. Why deny, efface or destroy them?
Besides, great painters know full well that their pigments will evolve
and their colours will alter; and they act accordingly. What they want
for posterity is not the original state of their canvas or panel but a later
one that they themselves will never see. So when we try to restore a

painting or artistic object to its original state, we may be contravening the wish of the artist. Historical reality consists in not only how things were originally, but also the effects of time. But to what extent should we allow time to do its work?

Documentation also presents another difficulty: today we see the images and colours of the past in lighting conditions very different from those of pre-twentieth-century societies. A flaming torch, oil-lamp or candle (whether tallow or wax) produces a light quite unlike that provided by an electric current. That goes without saying. Yet how much notice is paid to this fact by historians, visitors to museums or exhibitions, and connoisseurs of ancient art? None at all. Yet to ignore it sometimes leads to absurdities. Consider, for example, the recent restoration of the ceiling of the Sistine Chapel and the great efforts – both technical and on the part of the media – made in a bid 'to recapture the freshness and original purity of the colours applied by Michelangelo'. Such an exercise may stimulate curiosity even if it is found somewhat aggravating; but it becomes completely pointless and anachronistic if the layers of colour thus revealed are illuminated by electric lighting. What do our modern lighting systems really reveal of the colours of Michelangelo and his pupils? Is not the travesty even greater than that operated by the workings of time since the fifteenth century? It is even more alarming if one considers the examples of Lascaux or other prehistoric sites that have been destroyed or damaged as a result of the fatal encounter between testimony of the past and the curiosity of the modern world. On the other hand, though, it would be impossible or even absurd to reintroduce candles or oil-lamps in the Sistine Chapel. So what is to be done?

All the lighting of past times was produced by flames. These imparted movement to the forms and colours of images and paintings and animated them, making them vibrate, even lending them a kinetic quality (one has only to think of a document such as the Bayeux tapestry seen by the light of torches or candles). Our electric lighting, in contrast, is relatively static and imparts no movement to either forms or colours. So there is a considerable difference in perception between what we see and what our ancestors used to see. Like it or not, we never see an object, document or work of art exactly as they did. To an ancient, a medieval or even a more modern eye, colours were always in movement: Aristotle himself pointed out that colours always convey movement. For eyes today, colours no longer move, or hardly do; they seem immobile: the difference in perception is immense.

Similarly, nowadays we have no difficulty in lighting a large surface in a uniform manner. In a contemporary museum, a painting measuring 3 metres by 5 will have no part of it less lit than the rest. Thanks to spotlights and other increasingly perfected artificial lighting, a canvas can be perfectly lit in its entirety, without the picture's surface suffering in any way. Such a procedure was impossible for societies in the past. Whatever their nature and efficiency, lighting systems that depend on flames cannot illuminate a large surface evenly; there are always zones that are well lit and others that remain in the shadows. This accounts for the interplay of chiaroscuro, so relished by both artists and their public in former times. The arrival of electricity totally changed the relations of spectators to the objects of their attention, whether these were works of art, images or, perhaps even more, colours.

Another difficulty that explains that silence on the part of historians stems from the fact that, ever since the sixteenth century, they have been accustomed to basing their work on black-and-white documentation: at first, engravings; later, photographs. For nearly four centuries, 'black-and-white' documentation was all that was available for reproducing, studying and making known figurative evidence from the past, paintings included. In consequence, the modes of thought and sensibilities of historians seem likewise to have been converted to black-and-white. Relying on engravings, books and then photographs, the images of which were mainly black-and-white, historians (and perhaps art-historians in particular) have, until quite recently, thought about the past and studied it either as a world made up of greys, blacks and whites, or else as a totally colourless universe.

Recourse to colour photography in recent times has not really changed the situation. At least, not yet, despite the technical and documentary progress made in the past three or four decades. For one thing, modes of thought and sensibility are too deeply ingrained to change radically in one or two generations; for another, access to documentation in the form of colour photography has remained an inaccessible luxury for too long. For students, young researchers and even established scholars, even the operation of creating slides in a museum, library or exhibition has for a long time not been easy or has even been prohibited. Institutional obstacles would arise on all sides to discourage the researcher or extort money from him. Furthermore, for understandable financial reasons, the proprietors of reviews or scholarly publications have been obliged to ban colour-plates. In the university world, there has long existed a discrepancy between the potentials of state-of-the-art techniques (in the world of astro-physics or medical imagery, for example) and the traditional work of historians, who have to cope with numerous difficulties – of a technical, financial or institutional nature – in order to study the pictorial documentation that has come down to us from the past. And those obstacles have, unfortunately, still not yet been overcome, while the technical and financial difficulties that faced earlier generations have now been aggravated by unbelievable legal restrictions. If one is a historian, it is wiser to work with words than with images!

The more so, given that colour photography is a technique that still has its weaknesses. For example, it is impossible to photograph gold. As a medieval specialist, I discover this, to my cost, every day. Gold is at once matter, light and colour; so it needs to be photographed from three different angles. One of the many functions of gold on an object or a work of art, is to reflect light, set it in movement, make it 'speak'. Photography can only capture one single moment and therefore confines the gold to a static role. Moreover, trying to capture its colour is an unrealizable task: in a photograph, the gold will always be too yellow or too red, or even greyish or greenish. The same goes for stained glass: the photo fixes one single moment, whereas the stained glass is meant to come alive as the sun moves round and the seasons change; its colours are constantly shifting. So to study stained glass from photographic documentation makes very little sense.

Despite the technological progress of the last three decades, despite the existence of growing numbers of data-banks with increasingly numerous and diverse powers, and despite the millions or even billions of numbered images that can be consulted remotely, to me the future does not seem as radiant and colourful as it is claimed to be. What we gain on the one hand, we often lose on the other. The directors of public collections, those who hold the copyrights of images and the fanatical devotees of new techniques sometimes think, naively, that consulting a work of art or an ancient document on a computer screen dispenses with the need to make contact with the original. On the pretext that the work of art or document has been digitalized and that a reproduction of it is accessible on a data-base, those in charge may limit access to it or withhold permission to consult it directly. Where problems of colour and other matters too are concerned, this is crucial. Many of the item's aspects, issues and parameters are impossible to study on the screen of a computer. One simple example is provided by the contrast between a matt colour and a shiny one. For centuries, all European painters played on this opposition when constructing their paintings, differentiating zones and planes, creating meaning and producing aesthetic effects. For a spectator – and in particular for a historian of painting – distinguishing between matt colours and shiny ones is indispensable. But how can one even identify, simply identify, matt colours on a computer screen?

4

ON SPORTS GROUNDS

GOALS AND REFEREES

'You, fatty, get into goal!' This order, delivered in a menacing tone by a teacher of physical education, marked the start of my sporting career in the autumn of 1957. I was 10 years old, a pupil in the first-year class in a large *lycée* in the southern suburbs, constructed under the Second Empire; and, along with all my schoolmates, on two afternoons every week I benefited from the school's magnificent playing-fields, which occupied the flat area of a huge park. This was the Lycée Michelet, in Vanves. I had never actually played football but the role of goal-keeper immediately appealed to me. After a few months, I became the official goal-keeper for the school's first squad and I remained that for five years, first for the youngest group, then for the Juniors and then for the next age-group (aged 15 to 17). To tell the truth, our results were never brilliant. The sports at which Michelet most excelled were rugby, handball and swimming. In the course of five years I faced a considerable number of goal shots, maybe over a thousand. It is true that, in those days, 'floods of goals' were frequent in school matches, producing scores such as 6–4, 7–2, or 10–0. All the same, those 'floods' were nothing compared to the number of goals scored in the school playgrounds at lunchtime: in twenty minutes, it was common to reach astronomical

scores: 23–15, 32–26 or even higher ones. It is true that the surface of
our pitch was cement and our feet kicked around a bald, grey tennis ball
that it was almost impossible to stop. Two sad, misused satchels served
as goal-posts, despite our promises to our parents not to 'clown around
with our satchels'.

On the real football pitches, despite a number of memorable humili-
ations – mostly inflicted by that thorn in our flesh, the Lycée Lakanal
of Sceaux – I enjoyed the position of goal-keeper. There, on my goal-
line, I was a unique actor, as the shirt that I wore seemed to proclaim: it
was a different colour from those worn by the rest of the players in my
team. They, like all the young sportsmen who represented the Lycée
Michelet, were obliged every Thursday to don a black-and-white shirt
and black shorts. But I had a choice: either a red – verging on orange –
shirt, hooped with a white stripe, or else a green, slightly greyish one,
both of which had a large 'I' emblazoned on the back. I was magnificent. The rest of the team were not, committed as they were to black,
an unusual colour to find on the sports grounds of the Paris region.
They would have preferred a different colour, but black was the school
colour and possibly had been ever since the school was founded, certainly since the 1920s. Nobody had ever thought to change it or even
to point out to those in charge that such a colour was not suited to
children and adolescents. Right up to the day of my departure, in 1965,
all the teams representing the Lycée Michelet of Vanves were always
dressed like All-Blacks. I wonder if they still are.

It is true that in those days there was less confusion with the referees'
kit. In school matches, the referee would usually be a physical education
teacher, who would stick to his own professional uniform: generally a
track-suit dyed an ugly light blue that appeared in the mid-fifties and
was still in use twenty years later. I have seldom seen such an ugly garment, especially when the legs were shaped like tapering ski-trousers
and the colour, already nasty enough, took on a shiny, satiny look.

In those days, the compulsory black of referees was limited to important fixtures at national or departmental levels and was not seen at
school matches. It is not easy to date with precision the point at which
official football referees were regularly dressed in black: maybe around
1920–5, although some evidence suggests that it was earlier. Prior
to World War I, referees often wore a shirt with vertical black and

white stripes, as striped garments stood out more sharply than single-coloured ones. In some sports (boxing, baseball, basketball, ice-hockey and so on), particularly in the United States and Canada, referees continued for years to wear a similar striped kit. In other sports – rugby, for example – bright colours began to take over from stripes or plain black as early as the 1970s. In football this happened rather later.

Historically, in Europe, black had for centuries been the colour of authority, for both the police and the courts of justice. That is why, like the judge or the policeman, referees took to wearing black, unrelieved black, which never failed to impress both players and spectators. The man in black was intimidating and imposed respect, especially as he also carried a whistle – the primary attribute of a policeman – which gave him a rather military air that was unusual on a sports ground.

Later on, unlike policemen, customs officials and other uniform-wearers, football referees did not switch to navy-blue uniforms. They, like judges, remained 'men in black'. However, from the 1980s and 1990s on, the growing number of football matches shown on television gradually forced them to swap their black shirts for brightly coloured ones that stood out clearly from the shirts of the team players on the pitch. In France, referees dressed in yellow, green, pink and even white now made their appearance. The colours were attractive, of course, but they did not inspire respect. By abandoning black, referees forwent much of their authority, as is clear to see from the way that contemporary football has evolved, the increasingly numerous challenges and arguments and the threats of resorting to a video for decisions.

THE YELLOW BIKE

The navy-blue blazer of sinister memory, described in an earlier chapter, was not the first of my 'chromatic whims' (I think it was my Aunt Lise, who was like a second mother to me, who coined this quite accurate phase). A few weeks earlier, there had been the 'affair of the yellow bike'. I was a fairly spoilt child who had already owned several bikes, all of them green and all of them purchased from the same shop: Hamelin Cycles, in Alençon. The premises were pervaded by a particular smell that delighted me: a mixture of glue, rubber, oil and other mysterious products. For my thirteenth birthday, my father promised me a 'grown-up' bike, hoping that I would not grow much more and so would keep it for a long time. But instead of buying it from the usual shop in Alençon, he decided to go to a shop run by a childhood friend with whom he had recently met up: Ripault Cycles, in Saint-Pierre-des-Nids, a village in the north of the Mayenne region. The shop was quite small, with a quite different smell and a less varied choice than the Hamelin shop.

My father's friend welcomed us warmly, one July day in 1960. He had prepared for our visit by setting in the window a fine adult bike equipped with racing handle-bars. He hoped I would like it and thought that the handle-bars would win me over. It is true that none of my earlier bikes had had such dropped handle-bars that would make it possible to show-off on the roads of Maine and Normandy. The good fellow took me for a normal adolescent. He had no idea that I couldn't care less about the handle-bars which, in fact, I considered ridiculous, and he had no way of sensing that, for me, the most important element in a bike was not its shape or any accessory, but its colour. That was the determining criterion. And this bike was yellow. Not green, as I wanted, but yellow, and a bright yellow! Impossible to seat myself on such a machine, however much of a 'little beauty' it was.

There followed a discussion, rejection, arguments and threats: I voiced my 'chromatic whim', as usual. In the end I was denied a bike and left on foot. My father's friend was dumbfounded. Through my fault, he had not only lost the chance of a good sale but, on top of that, he could not understand how it was that the arguments he had used to win me over to the yellow colour of this (unsellable?) machine had failed to convince me. According to him, this yellow was the very colour of the yellow jersey of the Tour de France: everyone would admire me, take me for a champion, want to ride my bike. At this point he reminded me of the history of the yellow jersey, mentioned a few champions of the Tour de France (Robic, Bartali, Coppi, Kübler, Koblet, Bobet) and praised the talent of Jacques Anquetil whom, for my part, I had never admired.

Such quibbling left me cold. He did not go into who it was I might want to lend my bike to; and the only person I hoped to see perched on my bicycle luggage-carrier was a girl whom I greatly admired, who was a friend of my cousin. As for the history of the yellow jersey and the Tour de France honours list, I knew it all by heart since, for the past year, I had been reading the daily *Équipe* (as I still am, fifty years later). Even though my favourite sport was not cycling, but athletics, I could without hesitation reel off the names of the victors in the Tour de France and even the first five in the general classification, from 1903 onward. I furthermore knew, as no doubt did many adolescents of my age, that the yellow jersey had been created in 1919 so as to pick out the cyclist leading the Tour de France competitors at that point. The first to wear it was the legendary Eugène Christophe . . . who never did actually win the Tour de France.

In any case, I felt scant sympathy for this jersey. Not really because it was yellow – which was neither my favourite colour (which was green) nor my least favourite (purple) – but because it was awarded to a winner. In sport, I have never felt much admiration for 'winners' – and even less for winners on the field of battle or in the competitions of daily life. Winning, in itself, is not indecent, egoistical or futile (although, actually . . .), but to be proud of winning certainly is.

Why choose yellow as the emblem of the leader of the pack? Between 1910 and 1920, all the opinion polls already regularly showed that the colour was not much liked: in fact, it rated last in the six basic colours when people were asked about their favourite colour. In France and in Europe, from 1880 down to the present day, it retained that same position, despite the many technical mutations and transformations that occurred. The order still went as follows: blue, green, red, white, black, yellow, and it was the same for both men and women, whatever their ages and professions.

The history of the colour yellow in Europe is that of a lengthy depreciation. In Greece and in Rome it was a much appreciated colour that played an important part in social life and religious rituals. But in the Middle Ages, yellow underwent a devaluation. It became the colour of deceit and cowardice, then that of felony and infamy. It was presented as the colour of traitors in the *Chansons de Geste* (Ganelon) and in stories of the Round Table (perfidious knights). It was also the colour assigned to excluded or rejected individuals (Jews, heretics, lepers, convicts and so on), who had to display defamatory badges and clothing insignia. Finally, when associated with green or set alongside it, yellow became the colour of disorder and madness. To medieval minds, the only good yellow was the yellow of gold. In modern times, without shedding any of its negative characteristics (in fact far from doing so), yellow has also become the colour of sickness (even of death) and of jealous or deceived husbands. In the nineteenth century, yellow was associated with the idea of denunciation and treachery. In working-class society, it is the colour assigned to those who betray the class to which they belong: strike breakers, workers who refuse to take part in vengeful action, trade unions in hock to the bosses – and all those who stand in opposition to red trade unions and the partisans of revolutionary action. In the aftermath of World War I, yellow had a bad reputation, particularly in working-class circles.

In view of all this, why was yellow the colour chosen in 1919 to indicate to spectators who was the best placed to be victorious in the Tour de France? The answer is very simple: yellow was the colour of the paper on which the journal *Auto*, which organized the Tour de France, was printed. It was one of those dull, pale yellows then used for cheap paper intended for ephemeral uses or mass-consumption: in short, a yellow neither promotional nor prestigious. But the publicity campaign was soon to bear fruit and the Tour de France would do its magic. By the 1930s, this jersey had become almost a mythical fetish. It engendered a syntagmatic expression – 'the yellow jersey' – the use of which extended far beyond the domain of sport. There were – and still are – yellow jerseys in the world of finance, economics and politics. 'To wear the yellow jersey' has for close on a century meant 'to be the leader of the field', whatever the type of competition and the method of classification involved. And this is so not only in France but also in neighbouring countries, including Italy, despite the fact that the cyclist in the lead of the hotly competitive Giro d'Italia, which takes place in the spring, has, ever since 1923, worn a pink jersey (*una maglia rosa*). So the yellow jersey has played its part in promoting this unpopular colour and converting it into the colour of victory, or even excellence. It is no longer the dull yellow of the *Auto* news sheet, but a yellow that is luminous and dazzling, a kind of new gold.

All the same, in 1960 it did not succeed in selling a yellow bicycle to a stubborn adolescent who ardently desired a green one.

BARTALI AND THE ITALIAN FLAG

What is the greatest sporting exploit there has ever been? The six athletics records beaten or equalled in less than one hour by Jesse Owens at Ann Arbour on 29 May 1935? The unprecedented long jump (8.9 metres) of Bob Beaman in the Mexico City Olympic Games on 18 October 1968? The double victory of two skiers from Lichtenstein, the brother-and-sister pair Andreas and Hanni Wenzel, who won the the male and female cups for alpine skiing in 1980? I myself immensely admire the two final matches played out by the Australian champion Ken Rosewall at Wimbledon, the first in 1954 and the second in 1974: twenty years apart! Unfortunately, he lost both finals.

Curiously enough, although they are seldom in agreement, historians of sport – the genuine ones, who do separate sport from political, social or cultural history and do not concentrate solely and outrageously on the most recent years – seem to agree on the following point, even if many of them stress how difficult it is to compare different champions, periods and generations. Most of them agree that the greatest sporting exploit of all time was that achieved by Gino Bartali, the victor of the Tour de France in 1938 and then again in 1948. Considering all that happened in Europe and in the world between those two dates, his two successes take on an exceptional dimension.

I have always admired Gino Bartali (1914–2000). As a child, I preferred him to his rival Fausto Coppi, who was five years his junior. As an adult, I realized that there was a symbolic aspect to their rivalry. At the end of the war, each of them embodied the two faces of an Italy that was reconstructing itself: the one Catholic and traditional (Bartali), the other more in tune with a certain modernity (Coppi). More recently, soon after Bartali's death, certain documents that were published revealed his exemplary conduct during the war. Bartali helped to save Jews and fighters of the Resistance: he was a model of Justice.

He was also a 'proper' champion, perhaps the last of the great racing cyclists. The longevity of his career is remarkable: it began in 1935, when he became a professional, and lasted until 1954. So he was a quite exceptional champion and he would have achieved even more had the war not interrupted sporting competitions for more than five years.

Gino Bartali was a great favourite among journalists. Jacques

Goddet, the editor of *L'Équipe* for many years, treated him as a kind of cult figure, and the press was happy to record his comments, which were sometimes grumpy, often ironical and always pertinent. One of them unexpectedly concerns the history of colours. When, in 1952, at the age of 38, he became the champion cyclist of Italy for the last time, Bartali climbed up onto the podium, watched the raising of the Italian flag and was presented with a new tricolour jersey in green, white and red. He remarked to the journalists present that the green of the flag and of this new jersey was 'lighter than in the past'. When he was champion of Italy for the first time, in 1935, the green was dark, even greyish. In 1937 and 1940, for his second and third victories, the green had become lighter and had taken on a middling hue. But now, in 1952, it really was light, almost luminous.

There was nothing anecdotal about the great champion's remark. It can also be applied to other European flags and reflects general changes in sensibilities in the domain of colours. For example, a similar point could be made about the blue of the French flag. Between the wars, it was almost always a dark blue, and when I was a child, in the 1950s, it was still a navy-blue; a couple of decades later it was a little lighter, and today it is a frankly royal blue. In 1974, at the start of his seven-year term as president, Valéry Giscard d'Estaing had in fact publicly expressed his wish to see the blue of the French flag become lighter. And this was not a metaphor that could lend itself to glosses of a political nature, but a personal and aesthetic observation intended to be taken quite literally.

I remember being shocked by this presidential concern for a lighter blue. Not so much because I personally preferred – and still do prefer – dark blues to light blues, but rather because, as a historian of emblems, I knew that the colours of flags are colours that are abstract, conceptual and heraldic: nuanced shades do not count. The blue of the French flag, like the heraldic azure of ancient royal coats of arms, can be navy-blue, middling blue, sky-blue or slightly greenish or purplish: the different shades are of no importance or significance. What matters is the idea of blue, of white and of red. Besides, there is no constitutional text that defines the nuances of those three colours and when the tricolour flag flutters out of doors, subject to the effects of bad weather, it may undergo changing shades. However, this in no way alters the fact that it remains the French flag, a national emblem and a symbol of Republican liberty.

The same goes for most national flags, those of Europe as well as others throughout the world. There are a few countries (Uruguay, Israel, Qatar, Bahrain and a number of others) that define the colours of their flag by reference to a colour chart, but those that do so are generally developing countries or countries that have only recently won their independence. Such chromatic precision is not traditional where emblems are concerned since, in their case, the idea of a colour counts for more than its material or colouring. Like the French blue, the Italian green may take on a variety of nuances in different periods, with different colouring agents, textiles and climatic conditions. The fact that Gino Bartali, that exemplary champion, noticed it growing lighter in the course of his decades of victories, in itself constitutes historical evidence.

THE TOUR DE L'OUEST (THE WESTERN CYCLING TOUR)

I did not catch a glimpse of the Tour de France until quite late on, when I was about 20, in the late 1960s. It was in the north of the Mayenne region, in the depths of deepest France, amid one of the fairest countrysides ever seen. However, my memory of this occasion is neither very emotional nor very distinct – just an impression of a confused range of colours and a cacophony of sound that was hard to bear: the racing cyclists flashed past me at a crazy speed – impossible to pick out any particular jersey or to identify any of the cyclists – and the insistent din of the publicity cavalcade bordered on the intolerable. The wait had been long and pleasure was altogether absent. Some of the cyclist dreams of my childhood died at the edge of that country road, the departmental 121.

On the other hand, I cherish far more agreeable recollections of the late, lamented Tour de l'Ouest, an end-of-season competition that took in Brittany, the Vendée, Maine and Western Normandy and that was discontinued in 1960. It was not limited to the top professionals. Amateurs and semi-professionals could take part – often more imaginative and fearless competitors than those who took part in the Tour de France. Frequent attempts were made to lead the pack, and in each leg of the race the situation underwent many reversals of fortune. The *Ouest-France* newspaper published a detailed account of the race on the following day and provided exhaustive lists of the positions of the cyclists. I was just 10 years old and I perused them with delight. It was those interminable lists, printed on the mediocre paper of a local daily, that early in my life fostered my taste for lists and the structures of listing – a taste that endures to this day.

The earliest results that I remember date from 1957. The malicious quirks of sport and name-giving had ruled that in that year, for just a few days, the two competitors placed at the top of the list were called Bihouée and Bihannic, both Breton names, with an unforgettable ring to them. In the following year, I actually set eyes on those two competitors on their bikes, at Lambelle, in a post-Tour (de l'Ouest) rally: Edouard Bihouée wore a green-and-white jersey, Arthur Bihannic a red-and-white one.

My memory of cycling competitions in the late 1950s is constructed around champions and jerseys. The latter displayed bold colours and carried virtually no advertisements: only the team name – often linked, with a dash, to the names of the principal team sponsors – appeared, and did so in a relatively discreet fashion. The various jerseys were easy to recognize and had, for children in particular, classificatory values that today's jerseys, confused, gaudy and spattered with advertisements as they are, no longer possess. How can professional sportsmen agree to such humiliation, disguising themselves as many-coloured ham-actors and posing as live advertisements designed to glorify particular brands and products? What image do they have of themselves? Does the lure of profit annihilate all dignity? The fact is that, in France, some of the best-paid players earn in a single year a sum that a person on a minimum wage might not earn in 1,000 years! What has happened to the sober garments of the past, when sport was still sport and the presence of colour on cycling jerseys performed a triple role that was at once deictic (who is who?), aesthetic and magical?

In those days, most of those jerseys were two-toned, associating white with one basic colour (red, blue, green or yellow). Orange and purple were rare, and pink, grey and brown were even more so. Some jerseys were of a single colour, but the black-and-white cycling shorts or leggings conferred upon the costume the two-toned look characteristic of any emblematic outfit. What happy days they were, when jerseys in four or five colours did not exist and the synthetic textiles that nowadays make all bright colours glitter abominably had not yet appeared upon the scene. Everything was matt, true, uniform, almost heraldic.

COLOUR BY DEFAULT

Who remembers the colours of the first flavoured yoghurts that appeared in French dairy and grocery stores in the mid- or late fifties? My memory of them is relatively precise. They were Danone products, sold in glass jars and at first there were only three flavours: strawberry, banana and vanilla (raspberry, lemon and apricot appeared slightly later). The strawberry yoghurts were a deep pink and were topped by a red aluminium lid. Banana yoghurts were more or less yellowish but their lids were a fine golden yellow. As for vanilla yoghurts, they were white, like plain yoghurts, but their jar was closed by a blue lid. Why blue? Unlike strawberries and bananas, which naturally relate to red and yellow, there is no reason why vanilla should be associated with the colour blue. Brown or black would have been more suitable, so why that astonishing choice?

It was prompted by culture, not nature, and, as a choice, made 'by default'. A yoghurt with a brown lid, to evoke vanilla, would not have been attractive and would probably have been hard to sell. Safer to stick with the primary colours, which were still (though, alas, no more) revered everywhere in the 1950s, and as much in the domain of high artistic creation as in that of the designs and strategies connected with mass consumption. Red and yellow were already taken, so only blue was left to represent vanilla yoghurts. And that is what happened. As a matter of general convention, vanilla became blue and so it has more or less remained in quite a few classificatory lists of foodstuffs.

Far from being insignificant, that first selection for yoghurt pots illustrates the idea of choice 'by default', an essential notion, omnipresent in all codes and social practices involving colour. It is an idea that is both individual and collective and it accompanies us not only in our daily lives but also, ever since long ago, in the multiform world of emblems and symbols. As a result, it conditions many of our preferences, beliefs and sensibilities.

Consider a very different and earlier example, that of the Olympic rings. These were definitively fixed on paper between 1912 and 1914, but because of current events they did not actually get to flutter on the Olympic flag – a magnificent flag in both design and colour – until the Antwerp Games of 1920. Each ring represents a continent and has a colour of its own: red for America, yellow for Asia, black for Africa, blue for Europe and green for Oceania. The first three of those colours seem to have been chosen (by whom?) for more or less ethnic (and perhaps slightly racist) reasons: red for the continent of the 'Redskins', yellow for that of yellow-skinned peoples and black for that of black men. But the other two colours are trickier to interpret. Blue, associated with Europe, seems to be a long-standing cultural heritage: it has been the preferred colour of Europeans ever since the eighteenth century and is the one that the other cultures on our planet use as the emblem of Europe. Furthermore, in 1912–13, the colour white was not available for Europe's Olympic ring, as it had already been reserved for the background of the future Olympic flag. So blue it was, for Europe. But where did the green for Oceania come from? Why this association? What was it intended to convey? Oceania is linked with this colour by no particular relations, either natural or cultural. It is not heavily forested, and traditions – first native, then colonial – have never especially singled out the colour green. With hindsight, of course, attempts have been made to rationalize the association between green and Oceania by resorting to a number of explanations but, like all a-posteriori explanations, these have been fragile, if not fallacious.

For here too, it is a matter of a choice 'by default'. Five of the six basic colours were already taken – four for the first rings and white for the flag's background – so only green remained for the fifth ring. Oceania therefore became green and, as it happens, seems gradually to have become attached to the colour chosen for it by respectable English gentlemen who had never set foot on its soil and probably had no intention of doing so. In Oceania itself, this colour imposed from outside was first accepted, then positively claimed and finally proudly exhibited on its sports grounds. For example, Australia, probably the most sport-minded country in the world, often plays in green shirts, or ones that are partly green, even though this colour is absent from its national flag.

There are thus many colour-codes introduced in the nineteenth or twentieth centuries, in which the choice of certain colours is based on self-evident (or apparently self-evident) natural and cultural relations; and there are others in which the choices of colours seem totally artificial. The latter are in many cases due to selections made 'by default'. May we assume that such choices stem from what linguists call 'the arbitrary character of the sign'? It would seem so. And yet . . . is not a choice by default – that is to say, made by elimination – a choice that is motivated, fully motivated?

EASY COLOURS AND DIFFICULT ONES

Like streets, undergrounds, beaches, playgrounds and supermarkets, sports grounds constitute a special field of observation for a historian of colours. There, colours are omnipresent, not only on the pitch and the garments of the competitors but also on the terraces, on the badges, pennants, scarves and banners waved by their supporters. In some cases there is a long history behind those colours, not that either the actors or the spectators are aware of this. For example, who knows that the colours of the two prestigious football clubs of the city of Milan – the Inter (blue and black) and A.C. Milan (red and black) – were already in the late fifteenth century the colours of the banners of two particular Milanese quarters? Nobody. And yet those originally municipal, now sporting, colours have survived down the centuries, and today triumph on football pitches throughout the whole of Europe.

The colours to be seen in stadiums and sports halls are not just heraldic or emblematic. They can also constitute a code associated with the playing out of the game or competition. Skiing and judo provide good examples.

I have never practised judo. But I learnt to ski when I was very young, in a small skiing resort in the French Alps, which was then little known but is nowadays extremely popular: Notre-Dame-de-Bellecombe, in Savoy, not far from Mégève. In the fifties, the area of skiing pistes was less extensive than it is now, but the degrees of difficulty of the few pistes then open were already classified by colours: green for the easiest runs, blue for the fairly difficult ones, red for the difficult ones and black for the very difficult ones, which I, of course, never tackled.

I do not know where or when this code appeared or upon what

criteria it was based. Despite my research efforts, I have never come across any document that clearly explained when, by whom and why those colours were chosen and classified in that order. Such information as is to be found is contradictory. Only one thing is certain: this code was already in use in Austrian ski resorts in the late 1920s, in Switzerland in the early 1940s, and in France and Italy slightly later. Today, it is used in skiing countries throughout the entire world. What is the symbolic logic behind it? It seems to elude all comparisons and all explanations. Given that black was chosen as the colour of extreme difficulty, white, its opposite, should have been that indicating the easiest runs. However, white markers might be missed amid the snow, so another colour was chosen to indicate the easiest runs. But why green? Blue might have been what one expected. Not just because blue is in itself an 'easy' colour – that is to say, easy to use, consensual, unabrasive and upsetting to nobody – but also because, for European sensibilities, green has long been a much stronger, bolder colour and sometimes a rebellious and dangerous one. Why was this not taken into account? Was green considered to be awkwardly close to red, in a proximity that would have upset the all-too-fragile theory of primary and complementary colours (according to which green is red's complementary colour and therefore is the one most distant from it)? Was it a matter of scientific fantasies being preferable to symbolic traditions?

It is worth noting that some ski resorts make use not only of those four colours but also of two others: white and yellow – white, which may, as mentioned above, be hard to pick out, for indicating ski-pistes reserved for very young children; and yellow for those with a degree of difficulty in between those represented by blue and red. This positioning of yellow is exceptionally bizarre. What is it doing there, in between blue and red?

We may well find the classification of colours in the world of tatami mats even stranger, but of course here we depart from European traditions to encounter those of Japan – indeed another world! Judo is practised with bare feet and calls for a special costume: a *judoka* wears a suit of white cloth trousers and a loose but solid jacket that is kept closed by a belt that passes twice around the waist and is secured by a knot. The colour of this belt indicates the level of competence reached by the *judoka*. The hierarchy of colours is as follows: white (for beginners), yellow, orange, green, blue, brown and black. The black belt, which represents the top grade, is itself sub-divided into levels known as *dan* and numbered from 1 to 10. In Japan, at the 6th, 7th and 8th *dan*, the black belt is replaced by a white-and-red one; at the 9th and 10th *dan* level, it is replaced by a totally red one. This hierarchy of colours is a product of Japanese culture and it would be interesting to know how far back it goes. At any rate, it has gradually been adopted by all national Judo Federations as well as by the International Federation, created in 1952. The hierarchical colour system is thus identical for *judokas* the world over. Clearly, it takes a few liberties with the spectrum – a scientific classification of colours that was developed in Europe – and even more with Western symbolism (which, actually, takes no account of that spectrum). However, the differences are less great than might be expected. The two extreme poles are white and black: yellow functions as a semi-white and brown functions as a semi-black. Nothing, so far, to surprise a European. The place of orange though, between yellow and green, and that of blue between green and brown are more exotic. But most remarkable of all is the place of red, which acts as a superlative black. Japan, more subtle and inventive, places, in this 'beyond', red, the absolute colour.

The sporting hierarchy of colours for ski-pistes and that used for judo are thus different. Let us hope that television and globalization, those dreadful machines that crush all traditions and all cultures, never do fuse the two hierarchies and replace them by some degenerate code produced by the wretched alchemy of computers.

PINK AND ORANGE

I have already pointed out the distance that may separate a real colour from what it is called. Such differences are to be found everywhere, even on sports grounds. Take the example of rugby. At the start of the 2005–6 season, the prestigious Parisian team of the Stade français which, for more than a century, had played in either blue shirts or blue-and-red ones – the modern colours of the town of Paris – abandoned its old strip in favour of a shirt in which pink predominated, with blue or black facings and covered in logos and puerile and vulgar graphics. It was no doubt a way of underlining the switch to professionalism – a switch which, to my mind, has perverted and distorted rugby – and of engineering a considerable amount of publicity for itself. Pink has been rare on sports grounds generally, and even more so on rugby pitches: a team playing in pink was bound to be noticed, especially a team reckoned to be one of the best. But it was also a provocation, a bit of a swagger, for the new bosses of the Stade français seemed to favour this type of behaviour and to be trying to upset the customs of circles that they judged to be too traditional. I am by no means sure that such an attitude attracts sympathy or is even truly effective. In sport, novelty kills mythology; and without mythology, there can be no true sport. Any change in the age-old colour of a club's strip always reflects some failure and sometimes turns out to be suicidal – or, at the very least, contrary to the interests of that club.

All the same, in the eyes of a neutral observer, that is not the most astonishing development. The most astonishing lies in the identity of the principal sponsor of the Stade français: namely, the Orange phone company, the name of which is inscribed on the players' shirts. Actually, 'astonishing' is not really the right word; 'hilarious' would be closer to the mark – the shirt is pink or mainly pink and both its front and its back bear the inscription 'ORANGE' in enormous letters! This is a shirt which, in a few centuries' time will, like the *métro* ticket mentioned earlier, no doubt be intriguing archaeologists working on the practices and relics of our age. Faced with this pink object described as 'orange', they will be perplexed, just as I myself am perplexed faced with the comic effect of such a contradiction, which, however, in sports stadiums and elsewhere too, fails to make anyone laugh. Have those who frequent sports grounds become too serious or too greedy to burst out laughing at this involuntary and aberrant chromatic contradiction? Or, alternatively, is this a supremely cunning plan devised by sporting marketing agents? Have they done this deliberately so as to attract the attention of suckers and trample even more upon sporting values? If that is the case, they have been totally successful.

5

MYTHS AND SYMBOLS

LITTLE RED RIDINGHOOD

My interest in animals goes a long way back, to well before the thesis (*La bestiaire héraldique au Moyen Age*) that I produced on them while attending the École des Chartes (the School of Paleography and Archival Studies). My fascination developed when I was very young and was encouraged by the books that I was given at that time, the heroes of which were animals. Those books probably prompted my later research work into animal symbolism. They may also have been at the root of my attraction to colours. At a time when colour images were not as common as they are today, children's books constituted an inexhaustible reservoir of colours. And it was not just a matter of the illustrations in those books, for their titles themselves in many cases included a colour-term, as if the syntagma of 'the name of an animal plus a colour-term' was a way of attracting the attention of a child (or its parents) and making a sale: *The Blue Rabbit, The Orange Cow, The Yellow Duck, Little Brown Bear, The Nice Green Dragon*. In the presence of titles such as these, heraldry was surely not far off.

In the tales and fables themselves though, even if their titles did sometimes include a colour-term, references to colours were more rare. One had to read widely in order to gather a few together. For that very reason, the impact made by colour references is considerable and, like the stories themselves, these make up a heritage passed down from ancient times. It is concentrated primarily around the age-old triad of black–white–red, the three colours which, for centuries, if not millennia, have played the strongest of symbolic roles. The most obvious example is probably *Little Red Ridinghood*.

In this famous tale, the essential question concerns the colour: why red? Why a *red* ridinghood? It is, however, a question that few researchers have addressed. Yet this is a much-studied story, about which more or less everything seems to be known, in particular the fact that it originated long ago in Western medieval oral culture. In the Liège region, it was already documented around AD 1000, under the title *The Little Red Dress*. But, as is so often the case, the problem of the colour remains obscure. Why red? A number of obviously symbolic answers spring to mind: red prefigures the cruelty of the wolf, the murder of the grandmother and the blood that will flow. It is rather a cursory explanation, even if the wolf is assumed to be the Devil. Conversely, the idea that this red garment is a small magic cloak, a kind of *Tarnkappe* that will protect the little girl from the wolf's cruelty, is not false, but it too is inadequate. Adopting a somewhat anachronistic position, one might venture a more psychoanalytical interpretation: that red is the colour of sexuality – the little girl, on the brink of puberty, would very much like to find herself in bed with the wolf. It is a modern reading that has tempted a number of interpreters, in particular Bruno Bettelheim in his well-known work, *The Psychoanalysis of Fairy Tales*. Basing his remarks on three medieval versions of the story, transmitted orally, rather than on the sanitized versions of Perrault and the Grimm brothers, Bettelheim stresses the savage and sexual dimension of the story: the wolf invites the little girl to share a meal of the flesh of the grandmother whom he has just killed, and even to drink her blood; he then entices her into bed and has a different kind of carnal interchange with her – or, if it is not the wolf that violates the girl, the hunter does so, once he has dispatched the wolf. According to Bettelheim, the red symbolizes that twofold dimension of anthropophagy and sexuality. But did red really have a sexual connotation in medieval symbolism? I cannot be certain. Besides, as a historian, I am well aware that psychoanalysis is a tool of our own time, devised for our own time and not to be transferred, just as it is, into the past, especially the distant past.

Historical explanations may seem more solidly based, but they too leave us wanting more. Dressing young children in red was a long-established custom, especially in peasant circles; and that may be the simple origin for the little girl's red clothing. But it may be that, to pay her grandmother a visit, she dressed in her finest clothes – that is to say, as was often the case for the feminine sex in the Middle Ages, a red garment. Alternatively, this red may be explained by the particular day on which this tragic story unfolded: Whitsun, one of the greatest festivals in the Christian year. On this day the Holy Spirit was celebrated and, both inside the church and outside it, everything was decked out in red, the liturgical and symbolic colour of the Holy Spirit. The most ancient version of the story, dating from the year 1000, does not declare that it all took place on the day of Whitsun but, instead, that Whitsun was the little girl's birthday, which would account for red being her own special colour.

From a scholarly point of view, this last explanation certainly seems the correct one, but it has to be said that it is somewhat disappointing. All we have left are explanations of a semiological nature, based on the structure of the story and the threefold distribution of the colours involved. For red should be envisaged not on its own but as it relates to other colours that are either mentioned or suggested: the little girl clad in *red* takes a pot of *white* butter to her grandmother, who is dressed in *black* (her replacement in the bed by the wolf does not in any way alter the colour of the recipient of the gift). For ancient cultures, these were the three 'polar' colours, the ones around which most stories and fables that refer to colour are woven. For example, in the fable of the crow and the fox, a *black* crow drops a *white* cheese, which is then seized by a *red* fox; and in *Snow-White*, a *black* witch offers a poisoned *red* apple to a *white* girl. The distribution of the colours varies but they always operate around the same three chromatic and symbolic poles: white, red and black. Perhaps it is not possible to progress any further in our analysis.

LONG LIVE SCHOOL LATIN!

1 October 1957: for me, the first day of my first year at my secondary school, the Lycée Michelet, in Vanves, a huge public establishment in

the inner southern suburbs of Paris, founded under the Second Empire and possessed of a magnificent park, already mentioned above. In those days, no great distinction was made, as it is today, between the terms *lycée* and *collège*: for general education, the *lycée* covered everything from the *sixième* (the first form) right up to the final year. Furthermore, for one and all, including nursery and primary schools, the school year began on 1 October, a deeply Republican day that incorporated quasi-liturgical rituals.

So I took my place in the lowest class, lost in my Sunday-best clothes (or what passed for them) and assailed by deep emotions. Fortunately, my mother accompanied me in this necessary rite of passage and, like most other parents, she remained at my side until my name was called. At this point, I joined the group that was to form the future 'A/3' *sixième* class. The languages that I chose to study (or rather that my parents chose for me) account for that curious Alpha-numerical label: in the A/3 class, one 'did' Latin and German. It was a 'classical' class.

When my name was called out, I was given a precious and enigmatic piece of blue cardboard, which I was to keep with me all day. The blue indicated that I was in 'classics'; those who had chosen 'modern', that is to say who had, as early as the first year, rejected Latin, received a red piece of cardboard, which was already regarded as being more or less shameful, even if no such card was yet to be seen on the playing-fields. In those late 1950s, not only did every good pupil owe it to himself to learn Latin, but, for all those who entered upon the 'classics' path, Latin was and remained, from the lowest class right up to the top one, the major subject studied. Some readers may find it hard to believe that, half a century ago – that is to say, only yesterday – Latin was still the major subject in French public *lycées*. They may likewise find it hard to accept that in those years, and for a further decade, the most excellent pupils, those who came top in all subjects, for the most part proceeded to study literature rather than sciences. Yet that was truly the case. The Ecole Normale Supérieure Lettres was at that time far more prestigious than the Polytechnique.

This bothered me not at all. I never had to make a choice between literature and sciences or any reason to complain that Latin took up such a large place in secondary school studies: it was both my best subject and my favourite one. I have never abandoned it and, ever since that

1 October 1957, I have, either for pleasure or through necessity, read and translated Latin every single day. Sometimes I think about that piece of blue card that decided my fate for several decades. It was an important matter, not only for me but for all the pupils in my class: the blues had to go to one particular part of the *lycée*, the reds to another, and so it remained for the next six years. The Classics and the Moderns did not use the same classrooms, the same corridors or the same playgrounds. To tell the truth, they never mingled at all until the last year, which was perhaps just as well as they did not really like each other, as was evident in the annual rugby match between the Classics and the Moderns, which, without fail, degenerated into fisticuffs in the rain and the mud.

Today the question that most interests me is how this choice of blue for Classics and red for Moderns came about. Who made that choice, and according to what criteria? A brief enquiry told me that it was not confined to the Lycée Michelet but was also implemented in other public establishments in the Parisian region, the Buffon and Montaigne Lycées, for example. Was this due to some ministerial instruction or recommendation? But who was it, in the ministry, that regarded modernity as red and classical studies as blue? Some visionary? Someone who was colour-blind? A Sunday painter? A colour genius?

MY DISCOVERY OF HERALDRY

In my *lycée*, several of my teachers played an important role in the awakening of my tastes and interests and, later on, in the choices that I made upon leaving secondary education. First among them were the various Latin teachers who managed to get me to love a dead language soon to be threatened with abandonment in the school system. In what respect could the teaching of Latin bother the politicians who govern us? Jealousy? Rancour? Stupidity? Or was it a desire to turn pupils, right from the start, not into cultivated men and women but, instead, economic agents and to give them, at an early age, a taste for efficacy and profit? To achieve such an end, Latin was clearly not of much use. Nevertheless, for me, it procured great joy and led me to my profession as a historian of the Middle Ages. And that meant a great deal to me.

All the same, the teacher who played the major role in my years of apprenticeship was a professor not of Latin but of drawing. I was 12 years old and in the *huitième* (the third class) and, curiously enough, our teacher was neither boring nor heckling. He was a disciplinarian but knew how to interest his pupils. With him in charge, we did not spend six months of the school year trying to reproduce a plaster-cast of Gambetta on a piece of white cardboard, using a black crayon. In the drawing classes of the *lycées* of the Republic in those days, that exercise was a 'must'. It was a bust that, a few years earlier, some of the senior pupils had, for a joke, painted red; and it had never been properly cleaned. Incredible though it may seem, this thankless task of drawing Gambetta was one that I had to perform three times in the course of my school career: in the second-year class, in the fifth year and in the optional Baccalaureat drawing examination. Those were trying times for not particularly gifted young artists!

But nothing of that kind happened in my third-year class. Monsieur M… (I confess, to my shame, that I have forgotten his name), the drawing-master at the Lycée Michelet in Vanves, loved colour and tried to awaken his pupils to the various pictorial arts. At the end of the year, he had thus suggested that we produce a gouache painting of a splendid stained-glass representation of a coat of arms, of which he had brought along an enlarged photograph. It was a stained-glass window from the late fifteenth or early sixteenth century, probably of Swiss origin, which depicted ornate arms showing a large blue dolphin against a yellow background. The drawing of the animal was very stylized and gave it an aggressive air. The bright colours and schematic shapes pleased me enormously and, unlike François, the boy next to me, who was far more talented than I was but spent most of his lessons drawing parachutists on squared paper, I carefully tried hard to reproduce this attractive document. At the time, I knew nothing of the language of heraldry but, having preserved the modest painting that I had produced, I was later able to complete a full analysis of the heraldry of those arms: *d'or au dauphin d'azur, lorré, peautré, barbé et couronné de gueules, au chef de sable chargé de trois quintefeuilles d'argent* [Translator's note. This is a heraldic description. Roughly speaking, it translates as: yellow with a blue dolphin with fins (i.e. flippers), tail, barbels and crown in red, and a black chief (top horizontal band) bearing three silver cinquefoils]. A veritable little prose-poem. However, despite all my efforts, I never found any trace of this stained-glass window in any church, museum or civic building. But that was not the point. What mattered was the interest that the picture of this coat of arms portraying a dolphin aroused in me. The fact was that, even before I had completed my copy of the stained-glass window, I wanted to know more about the heraldry, the figures and the colours of which it was composed, and the rules that had to be respected in their representation. In short, I wanted to be initiated into heraldry. My first teacher was this drawing-master, who knew a bit about the subject. Apart from telling me the rudiments of what he knew, he gave me some advice as to what I should read and lent me a couple of books. These lacked any coloured pictures and seemed hard-going to me. Furthermore, the list of heraldic terms to learn was immensely long, seemingly unlearnable: over 1,000 words or more! I did little more than leaf through those two off-putting books. But in the various dictionaries and encyclopedias in my father's library, I found enough to satisfy my eyes and my curiosity: colour-plates accompanied by brief and intelligible captions. A colleague of my uncle, who taught history at the Lycée Henri-IV, completed my education in the domain of heraldry.

Soon I was able to use my pocket-money to purchase my first heraldic text-book, second-hand, possibly the best introduction ever written on the subject, *Le Manuel du blazon* (A Manual on Coats of Arms), by Donald Lindsay Galbreath, published in Lausanne in 1942. I remember that I found it in the Saffroy bookshop in Paris, in the rue Clément, and paid 35 francs for it. The price was relatively modest for a book that was already rare, but the owner of the bookshop was a friend of my aunt. This excellent work, very clear and with many illustrations, enabled me, three years later but still in the drawing class, to give a talk about it to my classmates. Not all of them gave me a hard time. Despite my clumsiness and shyness and aided by the teacher drawing on the blackboard, I managed to interest a few, and thus gave my first lecture on heraldry. I explained, in particular, that heraldry used only six colours, which were almost abstract, and that it classified them in two groups and used them in accordance with strict regulations. I shall be returning to this subject.

In that spring of 1960, I conceived a passion that has never left me, orienting my later studies, deciding my future and influencing my relationship to colours.

THE BLACK CAT

My parents were fond of cats and they had several. One was a big black cat called Dimitri, who lived for seventeen years. I have never encountered a cat more affectionate and placid. In the holidays, we used to take him with us to our holiday house in Normandy, in the Alençon region, not far from one of the most beautiful villages in France: Saint-Céneri-le-Gérei, where my father had lived in his early childhood during World War I. Our house was flanked by two farms, where my sister and I, both town-children, were happy to learn how to live among the animals of the countryside. The farmer 'down the hill' was a nice man but from another age. He was born around 1925 and died sixty or so years later, without ever having seen the sea, although it was less than 100 kilometres distant from his home. It is true that, when I was a child, these regions positioned on the edges of the Orne and the Mayenne, away from the major thoroughfares, were still living as they had at the beginning of the century. Some farms had only just been connected to the electricity grid, others were without running water, while yet others were composed of a single room where the farmer's family cohabited with the dogs, the poultry and, in some cases, the pig too. And this was in not 1910 or 1920, but the early 1960s!

Our neighbour was quite well housed, but in some of his habits he reflected those archaisms. Consider how he acted when he met our cat, which happened repeatedly as the lie of the land dictated that he had to cross our courtyard several times a day in order to get to his barn. In that courtyard, Dimitri, the most debonnaire of cats, would be warming himself in the sun or half-heartedly keeping an eye out for a field-mouse that he would never catch. He was a lazy cat. But he was black, and in those days, in the depths of the Normandy countryside, a black cat was still regarded as a creature of the Devil. That is why our neighbour made the sign of the Cross every time he encountered the animal. He also did so when he entered our kitchen and saw the cat asleep on a chair or by the fire. The sign of the Cross was believed to keep at bay the demons that inhabited an animal whose fur inevitably attracted the forces of Evil. A white, grey, brown or even reddish cat would not be a victim of such prejudices. On the other hand, a tabby cat might be and, similarly, would often provoke a sign of the Cross. In the underworld, stripes and the colour black were often coupled together. In Brittany, in that same period, around 1960, a sailor would never go to sea if, on his way to his boat, he encountered a black or a striped cat.

It was not just in Brittany and Normandy that such beliefs held sway. They were to be found in plenty of other regions of France, from which they have even now not totally disappeared. It is true that they originated in distant lands (but certainly not in ancient Egypt, where cats were revered). Many medieval documents testify to them. In the feudal period, for instance, the Devil and his demons were accompanied by a whole cohort of animals with dark fur or feathers, which also seemed to have emerged from the infernal depths. Some were monsters or hybrid creatures but others were real animals such as bears, wolves, owls, crows, goats or cats. In those days, the cat was not yet the domesticated animal that we know today. According to the bestiaries, it was a cunning and mysterious being that was deceitful and unpredictable. It stalked around the house or monastery, lived by night and frightened honest folk, especially if its coat was black. It was a creature of the Evil One and, like the latter, would flee at the sign of the Cross. For the purpose of catching rats and mice, weasels, more or less domesticated ever since the Roman Empire, were preferred to cats.

Later, the status of the cat changed for the better. It was allowed into the house, to warm itself by the fire, and became a faithful companion. But the fear of black cats persisted. At the time of the great witch hunts, at the beginning of the modern period, there were many stories that associated black cats with the witches' Sabbath, in which they were either major players or lent their physical form to witches so that these could participate in the occasion. Hence the sacrifices or burnings of cats that are well attested, even as late as the eighteenth century; and hence, too, a cruel practice that has still not completely disappeared from the depths of the countryside: the tails of black cats would be cut off, to prevent them attending the witches' Sabbath.

Even nowadays, a black cat may be a symbol of darkness and death. Its tail, claws and fur may still trigger irrational fears and repulsion, or veritable allergies. As for the eyes of a cat, they are believed to see in the dark and discover secrets never revealed to human beings or to other animals.

GREEN SUPERSTITIONS

However, black is not the colour that engenders the most numerous superstitions. Green is far in the lead here. There are people who would not, for anything in the world, ever wear a green garment. Others would refuse to accept the gift of an emerald, a gem-stone believed to bring bad luck. Yet others would not set foot in a boat with a green hull or even, more simply, one in which certain parts were painted green. A number of phobias involving green are still famous: for example, that of Michel Le Tellier (1603–85), the father of Louvois and Secretary of State for War, then Chancellor – probably the most powerful figure in France, next after the king and well ahead of Colbert. His fear of green was such that he banished it from all his dwellings, changed the colour of his coat of arms (the heraldic symbol of which was a *sinolpe* (green) lizard) and banned the use of green in all regiments fighting for Louis XIV, including foreign ones. More famous still, though, is the phobia suffered by Schubert, which has become positively proverbial. This great musician declared that he was 'prepared to go to the ends of the earth to avoid this accursed colour'. The life of Schubert, cut short at the age of 31, in 1828, was such a succession of griefs, failures and sufferings that one may well wonder if that fear of green, a colour that it is not possible entirely to avoid, was not, in truth, justified.

I, for my part, learnt of this belief in the curse of green in unusual circumstances, on the occasion of a wedding in the countryside at the beginning of the 1970s. The bride wore a classic white dress and the bridegroom was dressed unostentatiously in black and grey. His mother, a huge woman, wore an extravagant dark plum-coloured hat, adorned by many flowers. But the danger lay not in this strident head-piece of hers, but in the costumes of two cousins (or friends) of the bride, a father and son, possibly hunters, who presented themselves wearing green jackets and grey trousers. The comment of one of my friends, better initiated into this society of minor nobility in the Penthièvre region, which was devoted to traditional values, was: 'Elegant but deadly'. Intrigued by his comment, I asked him in what respect such green or greenish garments could be unlucky. He told me that proper behaviour ruled out the wearing of this colour on the occasion of a wedding: it would inevitably lead to harm to the young couple or their descendants. He went on to assert that, on such a day, at the wedding feast, no green vegetables should be served – with the exception of artichokes, a lucky vegetable, believed to be an aphrodisiac – nor should that colour green ever be mentioned. I was flabbergasted: not only because I had discovered that my favourite colour had such a negative reputation but, perhaps even more, because I realized that a friend of my own age, a good sailor and an excellent tennis-player and inveterate fisherman, knew of such superstitions and, furthermore, believed them.

I do not know whether the two indicted jackets harmed the couple whose wedding we were celebrating. But later on I had several opportunities to register how widespread the fear of green was. For example, my searches for a dark green pullover often ended in failure, for menswear shops seldom stocked such an article. A salesman explained to me that there were not enough blonde men in France to justify the sale of such a colour. It is true that it is one that is worn more often in the northern countries of Europe, where men with blonde hair are more numerous, as is testified by the famous 'British green' of the Shetland pullovers that were fashionable in the 1960s, and the green monochrome garments that are easily to be found in large German and Austrian stores. Actually, this discrepancy between France and Germany is by no means recent. A perceptive observation made by the great Protestant scholar, Henri Estienne, in 1566, upon his return from the Frankfurt Fair, reveals that it already existed in the sixteenth century. At that time, green was fashionable in Germany, whereas in France it was reserved for servants or buffoons:

If one saw a man of quality dressed in green, one would deduce that his mind was a bit wayward; whereas, in several places in Germany, such clothing appears to be acceptable. (*Apologie pour Hérodote*, ed. P. Ristelhuber, Paris, 1879 (I, 26))

All the same, if French clothing stores, still today, sell very few green garments, it is not just because of a hair colour. It is also, and above all, because green does not sell well, on account of the beliefs by which it is surrounded. Among men, but even more among women, this is a colour that is believed to be unlucky. Quite a few retailers of garments for women have confirmed to me that green dresses 'are hard to shift'. One of them, working for an important Parisian label, even went so far as to say that, in the eyes of some clients, 'a green dress is that of a witch'. Those comments from ready-to-wear retailers might well be borne out by jewellers, who are certainly aware that emeralds, despite their undeniable beauty, are gems that are hard to sell.

About twenty years ago, I made a modest contribution to this file of superstitions surrounding the colour green, in a little study of the curse of green in the theatre world. Actors do not like to be dressed in green, being of the opinion that this colour will be detrimental to the spectacle, if not to themselves personally. A similar tradition seems to exist in the publishing world, where it is said that a book with a green cover will not sell well. The few historians who have addressed these matters and have tried to discover their origins have, for the most part, concentrated on the Romantic period. Lighting, at that time, was not yet electric but was no longer as it was in the preceding century. It turned all green tones into a pallid and disquieting colour – hence their unpopularity on the stage. But, in my opinion, we should look further back. In the theatre, the fear of green was already well established in the mid seventeenth century. One unsubstantiated legend even asserts that Molière died clad in green clothes.

In fact though, the fear of green in the theatre was probably due to a problem of dyes. On baroque stages, the custom often was to distinguish between the main protagonists in a drama by means of a single-colour costume, so each character was dressed in a different colour. In the seventeenth century, however, dying fabrics green was a difficult operation, mainly because the mixing of blue and yellow was not a common procedure. The rules of the dyeing trade were, at that time, strictly distinctive and regulated: if one's profession was to dye things blue, one did not have a licence to dye things yellow, and vice versa. For this reason, vats of blue dye and vats of yellow were not to be found on the same premises, so it was not possible to plunge a piece of material first in a vat of blue dye, then in a vat of yellow. Green was obtained by other means, using vegetable colouring agents, but it remained dull, pale and greyish. This did not matter much as it was not a fashionable colour, except, that is, in the theatre, where certain roles were supposed to be associated with it.

In order to obtain a genuine, bright, luminous green, men working in the English and Spanish theatres had the idea of borrowing a colour that painters used: verdigris, a particularly toxic pigment obtained by pouring vinegar or acid onto strips of copper. They then applied this onto certain actors' costumes. and even onto certain items of stage scenery. Between 1600 and 1630, several actors died as a consequence of poisoning, but nobody really understood that the green paint on their costumes was the cause of this. The notion that soon spread was that green was an accursed colour and it began to be banned from theatres.

In the nineteenth century, the curse of green was still a matter of concern. But now it was not so much a matter of the verdigris obtained from copper and vinegar, as of that based on arsenic. Products obtained from this element were used in the production of green dyes and paints employed in interior decoration and on furniture, clothing and other objects in daily use. Such products, often odourless and tasteless, are extremely dangerous as, under the action of humidity, the arsenic tends to evaporate. This caused numerous accidents and increased people's distrust of the colour green. Napoleon may have been a victim of such poisoning on the island of Saint Helena. No serious historian these days thinks that the emperor was deliberately poisoned, but a number of researchers have pointed out that the furnishings in the house where he lived were upholstered in a green material – green being his favourite colour. The dye used was the dangerous 'Schweinfurt green' that was obtained in 1814 by dissolving slivers of copper in arsenic. This no doubt explains the presence of arsenic in the deceased emperor's hair and under his nails.

From 1860 onward, distrust of the colour green sometimes turned into a phobia. Queen Victoria, for example, developed a horror of this colour and banned it from all her royal palaces, most noticeably from Buckingham Palace where, I am told, it has never reappeared.

THE COLOUR OF DESTINY

As historians know, the bad reputation of the colour green dates from ancient times. It was already present in ancient Rome and seems to have become more acute in the Middle Ages: in the feudal period, green was the colour most favoured by the Devil and his creatures, who preferred it even to black or to red.

Yet when one looks into the matter and tries to assess the symbolic history of green in Western societies, it becomes clear that green was not so much the colour of evil or bad luck, as that of destiny. Like all other colours, green is ambivalent: it is the colour of both fortune and misfortune, both good luck and bad luck, and both hope and despair. Hence its links with practices and rituals in which chance is at work and one competes to win. For example, gaming tables have been green ever since the sixteenth century, when cards, dice, pawns, hopscotch and billiards were all already played out against a surface of this colour. As time passed, green became the emblematic colour of gamblers, of the places where they gathered, of the objects that they handled and even of the words that they used. In the first half of the following century, in French 'la langue verte' (green language) designated the technical slang of gamblers playing with cards or dice, as spoken in taverns and gambling dens. Later, under Louis XIV, the green surfaces used by gamblers moved from the underground world into gaming houses of a more aristocratic nature and even into the courts of kings and princes. Now pawns, dice, cards, money and stakes were all deposited on the green surfaces of gaming tables. That is still the case today, whether in palatial casinos or on the trays provided in the most unassuming of cafés.

Similarly, today most sports grounds are green, just like the meadows of the Middle Ages that were the venues for not only tournaments but also duels and the ordeals that decided the fates of those accused of crimes. But it is not a matter simply of grass and the colour of grass, for certain sports take place not outdoors, on growing grass, but indoors, on constructed surfaces: floor-boards, a carpet or linoleum. These surfaces are often green: here grass has been replaced by a variety of different materials. Table tennis (or ping-pong), perhaps the best example, is played on a table that is almost always green, clearly reflecting the highly symbolic link between a sports field and the surface on which a game is played. Whether the surface played on is meadow grass, the felt of a roulette or bridge table, a grassy football or rugby pitch or a wooden ping-pong table, the destiny of the competitors is thus associated with the colour green. Similarly, the administrative bodies that decide the fates of businesses and their employees meet on a 'green carpet'. In the presence of green, 'les jeux sont faits', and the stakes in such gaming may be considerable.

We may well wonder about the reasons for this symbolism and its origins. Why has green for so long been so closely linked with the idea of destiny, chance, gambling and fate? Why is it most often the colour of all that is unstable, all that changes, all that one loves or ardently desires but that turns out to be chancy, fleeting or inaccessible, starting with love or money (the famous 'greenback' springs to mind). To try to answer that question is to pose the huge problem of the relations between chemistry and symbolism within a particular society. In Europe, green for a long time remained the colour that was the most unstable chemically. For centuries, European dyeing and painting struggled to fix it – not to produce it but to stabilize it. This chemically unstable colour was regularly associated with all that was symbolically changing and ephemeral: youth, love, chance, fortune, hope . . . Could it be that this colour symbolism was quite simply engendered by the chemistry of pigments and colouring agents?

FURLING THE COLOURS

I have already described how it was that ordinary red trousers had brought about the temporary exclusion of two *lycée* classmates in the winter of 1961. A few years later, in a very different context, I noted if not a rejection, at least a distrust, of the colour red. This happened during my military service, in a period of training that took place in Draguignon, where the 19th artillery regiment was stationed. It was a difficult five weeks, not because of barracks life but by reason of the scorching heat that prevailed in Provence throughout the August of 1974. Among the various tasks assigned to the conscripts was attendance at the hoisting and lowering of the colours. This ritual required the combined efforts of three people. I was assigned to this task in the very first week, perhaps because I was the eldest in the group of 'scientists' in the contingent that had just arrived. Nobody could have known of my interest in emblems and colours or that I had recently defended a thesis devoted to coats of arms. I knew nothing about flags and was grateful for the advice that a seasoned comrade offered me.

He showed me how to hoist the colours and then how to lower them. Unfortunately, though, he did not show me how to furl them. On the first evening I did my best but it was a hit-and-miss kind of best, clumsy and almost an insult to the colours of France. A gruff sergeant told me off for it: 'One does not furl the tricolour as if it is a scout's necktie or a Hermès scarf.'

A few days later, a young lieutenant who had been watching me showed me how I should proceed. I carefully registered what he said. In the first place, the folds had to be made by winding the material round underneath, a difficult procedure that made it impossible to obtain neat, smooth folds and eventually made one inclined to give up the struggle and roll it all into a ball. Secondly, and more importantly, once the flag was furled, only the blue was supposed to be visible. The red and the white were supposed to be wrapped inside the blue, which served to envelop them. At a pinch, if the flag was not very big, a small area of white might be glimpsed on the edge of the rectangle obtained but, above all, the red must not be visible. When the flag was furled, the red had to disappear.

I do not know how this custom originated, but it seemed to convey quite a lot about the political and military symbolism of the colour red. The French flag, which appeared in the course of the French Revolution, sprang from the tricolour cockade that appeared in the days following the storming of the Bastille. One legend, fuelled by La Fayette's *Memoirs*, explained that the three colours of the cockade combined the colour of the king (white) with the colours of the town of Paris (blue and red). But that is a simplistic and probably false explanation. At the end of the eighteenth century, white was the colour that represented the king only among the military, and the colours of the town of Paris were not blue and red, but red and brown. All the documentation confirms this. It is probably in the nascent United States of America that we should seek the origin of the blue, white and red tricolour, which signalled support for new ideas and the ongoing Revolution. But perhaps we should not seek to know exactly how the French flag came to be: any flag that is not shrouded in a mystery concerning its origins forfeits much of its symbolic power.

However that may be, a tricolour flag was created for the French navy as early as 1794, but it was not until 1812 that the French flag as we now know it was adopted by the land forces. It did not become a definitive emblem of France until the July Monarchy. At this point, the stripe that was positioned next to the flagpole was the blue one (previously this was just as likely to be the red), but for several further decades the white stripe was wider than those of the other two colours. Does this mean that when the flag was furled, the white stripe enveloped it? If so, at what point did the blue stripe take over that role? And why? Today, the three components of the flag are usually represented by rectangles all of the same size; but occasionally the blue rectangle is wider than the two others. France uses a tricolour flag but its true national colour is blue, as numerous practices testify: for instance, on sports pitches the French are 'the Blues'.

Red, for its part, is the least prominent colour. It is only clearly visible when the flag is flapping in the wind and this is strong enough to display the three colours horizontally and fully. For the rest of the time, when the flag is not agitated by the wind or when the colours are furled, the red stripe is not visible. All that can be seen is the blue, or sometimes the blue and a little bit of white. Could it be that France is ashamed of the red part of its flag?

A HISTORICAL OBJECT THAT IS ALARMING

Let us remain in the domain of flags for a while. I have often come across them in the course of my researches, but have never devoted a serious study to them, even though they must be of the greatest interest to any historian of colours and emblems. The fact is that flags are historical objects that scare me; so I have always turned cravenly away from them. Nor am I alone in doing so. Not many serious studies are devoted to them. Why? Is it because many of them emerged from bloodshed? Or because the military and nationalistic rituals that they occasion seem alarming and dangerous? Unlike other national emblems or state symbols, flags still await their historians. Flags seem alarming because their use is so deeply and excessively anchored in the contemporary world that it is almost impossible to step back far enough to try to analyse how they function. Above all, they are alarming because, as has happened in the past, the attachment that some feel for them is still capable of giving rise to all manner of partisan appropriations, to every

kind of perverted usage, to all the passions and to every kind of devia-
tion, as plenty of political, ideological and social factors remind us daily.
So it seems advisable to speak of flags as little as possible.

In Western Europe, certainly, they are seldom mentioned in the
humanities. And I am not certain that this is altogether to be deplored.
Historiographically, there exists a patent link between totalitarian
regimes and periods and scholarly works on state symbolisms and
national identities. The scant interest that European democracies
have long evinced for such matters seems to me rather reassuring.
Conversely, and for the same reasons, I am not sure that we should welcome the increasing interest in such questions that has recently been
manifested by certain politicians. For their interest is neither neutral,
nor innocent, nor accidental.

At any rate, a history of flags has yet to be written – not a history of
this flag or that one, but a general history of flags seen as a set and forming a particular system of signs. This explains why the discipline that
is devoted to them – vexillology – has no scholarly status anywhere. It
seems to be everywhere left to connoisseurs of militaria and collectors
of insignia. The latter certainly devote many monographs, periodicals
and lists to them, but those publications are of little use to researchers:
the information is incomplete, contradictory and untrustworthy, the
scholarship often naive. Above all, there is no indication of an approach
that would envisage a flag as a social factor in itself. Vexillology is not
yet a science.

A flag nevertheless constitutes a topic for study which, in many
respects, is very rich. Flags are at once emblematic images and symbolic
objects and are governed by a strict code of rules and specific rituals
that lie at the heart of the liturgy of nations or states. But flags are not
present in all periods, nor in all cultures. Even if we restrict ourselves to
Western culture considered in the long term, there arises a whole sheaf
of questions that have not as yet prompted any serious studies.

Since when, for example, have men based their emblems on colours
and geometry? Since when, in order to do so, have they fastened a piece
of fabric to the top of a pole? Where, when and how did such practices,
at first more or less tentative and circumstantial, become transformed
into codes in their own right? What shapes, designs, colours and combinations have been adopted with a view to organizing and controlling

these codes? And, above all, when and how was the switch made from real fabrics, fluttering in the wind and designed to be seen from far away, to non-textile images that express the same emblematic and ideological message but are imprinted on surfaces of a wide range of materials? What material, ideological and social mutations have been involved in this evolution from flags, as physical objects, into flags as conceptual images?

Finally, in the cases of each flag, considered in isolation, what colours or combinations of colours came to be chosen? What was the flag supposed to signify? Who made that decision, and in what context, and why and how? And, once such a choice was made, how long did it last, how was it diffused and how did it evolve? Every flag has a history, and that history is seldom static. Who looks at a flag? Who knows or recognizes the flag of his own country, those of neighbouring countries, those of countries far away? Who knows how to describe them, represent them, passing on from the object to the image and from the image to what it symbolizes? These are just a few of the questions that no-one seems ever to have asked.

PLAYING CHESS

On my first visit to East Germany – the sad colours of whose atmosphere I have evoked above – in a park in Berlin, the name of which escapes me, I noticed some elderly, poorly clothed men playing chess on rudimentary chess-boards. These were unpretentious, more or less square planks of wood on which only the lines forming the sixty-four requisite squares had been traced. The chess-pieces, although much worn, were perfectly ordinary white and black ones, but the squares on the chess-board were not the usual black and white: they were all the same colour since each was indicated simply by lines roughly drawn on the wood, using an ordinary pencil. I was fascinated and watched the players for hours, noting that not only did they play in a strangely orthogonal manner (the castles, right from the start, being moved much more frequently than the bishops), which was, to put it mildly, unusual, but, furthermore, they took a long time to think before making each move. In a proper match, they would soon have been knocked out by a drastic *Zeitnot* (time constraints).

I had myself been a chess-player and, as I grew older, had become a historian of the game, but I confess that I had never played on such a chess-board, either in friendly games or in university competitions. So I do not know what it feels like to play the game on such a board. But I could make a rough guess, as I knew that the two-tone structure of alternate squares of the chess-board had not always existed. Several Indian and Persian miniatures and numerous medieval European images show chequer-boards on which the squares are formed simply by inter-crossing horizontal and vertical lines. The lines were one colour (usually red), the squares another (white or yellow). It is true that, in a game of chess, squares in two alternated tones are not compulsory or even strictly necessary. On the other hand, such a lay-out does help a player to visualize future moves and makes it easier to construct a diagonal tactic using the two bishops. Without such a lay-out of squares, a player requires extreme powers of concentration and geometric vision that most players today, unlike those in that Berlin park, no longer possess. However, the reason why the latter took so long to make their moves was probably the single-coloured nature of the chessboards that they used, and their consequent need to project upon those identical squares an imaginary alternating pattern of colours.

Actually, that alternation had not always been formed by white and black squares, even if the association of black and white presents the most emphatic of contrasts to a modern Western eye. Likewise, the chess pieces had not always been divided into opposing camps of white and black, for chessboards for many years used other pairs of colours. When the game originated in northern India in the early sixth century of the Common Era, it set a red camp in opposition to a black one and, in the eighth century, when the Muslim culture appropriated the game, it retained those two colours. On the other hand, once the game arrived in Europe, just before the year 1000, it had to be Westernized, that is to say not only did the nature and the moves of the pieces need to be rethought, but so too did their two colours. Red against black meant nothing to a feudal Christian mind. So the black was changed to white, and on the chessboard a red camp was opposed to a white one, for red and white at that time constituted the strongest contrasting pair.

The fact was that, for many years, the Christian Middle Ages had been constructing their colour systems around three poles: white, black and red – that is to say, white and its two opposites. But, unlike in the situation in Asia, those two opposites to white were not related in any way: they were neither opposed nor associated. In the year 1000, the pair of colours chosen for chess was white and red, a combination at that time predominant in emblems and in colour-coding practices. Three centuries later, however, that choice was questioned and gradually, in the course of the late thirteenth century and the fourteenth, the idea that the white–black pair was more effective than the white–red one came to predominate. In the meantime, the colour black had undergone a remarkable promotion: from being the colour of the Devil, death and sin, it had turned into the colour of humility and temperance, two virtues then fast gaining wider recognition. At the same time, Aristotle's theories on colour classification had been widely diffused and, according to these, black and white constituted the two extreme poles in all systems. Accordingly, in many domains the opposition between white and black came to be regarded as stronger and more meaningful than that between white and red.

Chess, a game both speculative and philosophical, was inevitably affected by these changing systems of thought. On chessboards, red pieces progressively gave way to black ones, and red squares were replaced by black ones: the game of chess was now ready to enter the black-and-white world that was soon to characterize European culture in the modern era. Indeed, alongside printed books, engraved images and the Protestant Reformation, the game of chess possibly contributed in its own small way to setting in place this black-and-white world and its aesthetic mutations. Still today, what could be more 'black-and-white' than a chessboard?

WITTGENSTEIN AND HERALDIC COLOURS

Ludwig Wittgenstein (1889–1951) was one of the greatest philosophers of the twentieth century. Not until after his death was this realized, for many of his works were published posthumously. Among them were the notes that he had made at the end of his life, in preparation for a study on the relations between colours and language. These notes were collected together and published for the first time in Frankfurt, in 1979, under the title *Bermerkungen über die Farben*; an English version had appeared in 1977 (*Remarks on Colour*, Oxford: Blackwell). This document contains a number of collections of sentences and statements, formulated in a disorderly and partly incomplete fashion.

Despite their rough or incomplete nature, a number of Wittgenstein's reflections seem to me fundamental, especially those that touch upon the philosophy of language: all of them underline the extent to which, when trying to think about colour, we are trapped by words. Others, though, I regard as more questionable, in particular those that concern the materiality of colours or their artistic properties: 'Adding white to a colour diminishes its colouration'; or 'Black deprives a colour of its luminosity; there is no luminous black' (*kein leuchtendes Schwarz*). On this last point, we should remember that many painters, starting with Velásquez, Manet and Soulages, knew how to produce particularly brilliant and luminous black tones.

Other remarks and formulations are astonishing – this one, for example: 'Why could shining black and matt black not bear the names of different colours?' Was Wittgenstein unaware (or pretending to be) that they *do* bear different names in a number of Indo-European languages, first and foremost Latin? In both classical and medieval Latin, *niger* means a shining black, *ater* a matt black; any novice Latinist (and Wittgenstein certainly was one in 1900, in Vienna) knew that. The same was true of Middle English (and most ancient Germanic languages): *black* was the word for a luminous black, and *swart* (close to the modern German *schwarz*) the word for a matt black. Shakespeare distinguishes between the two terms in several of his plays.

I find particularly touching another remark which, as phrased by Wittgenstein, seems like a hypothesis. It runs as follows:

> If there were a theory of colour harmony, perhaps it would begin by dividing the colours into groups and forbidding certain mixtures or combinations and allowing others. And, as in Harmony, its rules would be given no justification. (*Bemerkungen über die Farben*, 1, 67; *Remarks on Colour*, I. 74)

Without being aware of it, or pretending not to be, Wittgenstein, using different words, formulates the rules governing the use of heraldic colours, which dated from the twelfth century. It is strange that this philosopher, who was born and grew up in Vienna and then studied and taught for a while in Cambridge – both towns where examples of coats of arms abound – never investigated heraldic colours or the rule governing their association (rules that were both extremely strict and of unknown origin). Perhaps though, the snippet of words that has come down to us was just an introduction to a longer passage, never actually written, on the subject of heraldic colours. But we shall never know.

Usually, a coat of arms used only six colours, and in French and in English these bear special names: *or* (yellow), *argent* (white), *gules* (red), *sable* (black), *azur* (blue) and *vert* (green). It is worth noting that these are the six basic colours of the European culture. These heraldic colours are absolute, conceptual and immaterial: their shades count for nothing. In the coats of arms of the king of France, for example, which are '*d'azur semé de fleurs de lis d'or*' (azure strewn with golden lilies), the blue background can be sky-blue, a middling blue or navy-blue and the lilies can be lemon-yellow, orangey yellow or golden: such nuances are of no importance and mean nothing. The artist is free to translate that *azur* and that *or* as he sees fit, depending on what kind of material he is working on, the techniques he is employing and the aesthetic preoccupations that inspire him. As time passes, the same coat of arms may thus be represented using quite different shades of colour, but will nevertheless remain the same.

However, that is not the only peculiarity of the six heraldic colours. They fall into two groups: the first comprises white and yellow; the second comprises red, black, blue and green. The fundamental rule governing the way the colours are used forbids the juxtaposition or superposition of any two colours belonging to the same group (except where unimportant details are concerned). Take the case of an escutcheon showing a lion. If the background of the escutcheon is red (*de gueules*), the lion may be white (*d'argent*) or yellow (*d'or*) but it may not be blue (*d'azur*), or black (*de sable*), or green (*de sinople*), since blue, black and green belong to the same group as red. Conversely, if the background of the escutcheon is white, the lion may be red, blue, black or green, but not yellow. This fundamental rule dates right back to the origins of coats of arms and was respected always and everywhere (infringements of the rule seldom involve even 1 per cent of the coats of arms in a given collection). It is thought that the rule was borrowed from banners – whose influence over the earliest coats of arms was considerable – and that it was primarily linked to matters of visibility. The first coats of arms, all with two colours, certainly were visual signs designed to be seen from afar; and when seen from a distance, red is more distinct when the background is white or yellow than when it is blue, black or green. But these questions of visibility do not suffice to explain the problem as a whole, for this is also affected by the extremely rich colour-symbolism of the feudal period, symbolism which at that time was undergoing many changes.

The new society that was set in place in Western Europe following the year 1000 adopted a new order of colours: white, red and black were no longer the only basic colours, as had often been the case in Antiquity and the early Middle Ages; now blue, green and yellow were promoted to the same rank both in social life itself and in all the social codes attached to it.

The rule governing the use of heraldic colours has, down through the centuries, influenced other sign-systems – flags, military and sporting insignia and signboards (in particular, traffic signals). This rule was a veritable 'harmony', in Wittgenstein's sense of the word: a harmony that was at once grammatical, pictorial and musical. How could that great philosopher, so knowledgeable in so many domains, have remained unaware of this?

6

ON TASTES AND COLOURS

AN AMERICAN GIFT

The finest gift I ever received was presented to me by my grandmother's eldest sister, my great-aunt Aline. She was the widow of Henry Caro-Delvaille, the painter, a fashionable portraitist before World War I and a friend of Edmond Rostand, whose villa at Cambo he decorated before he became a society painter in the United States. He died in 1928. My great-aunt lived in Los Angeles and seldom came to visit her sisters in Europe. There were five sisters, all born between 1876 and 1884 into a bourgeois family in which the nature of their studies was decided by the order of their births. Aline, the eldest, had been to the École Normale and had graduated in classical literature, one of the first women in France to do so. She wrote several novels, including one best-seller, in the 1920s: *Ce charmant Thaddée Svenko* (The Charming Thaddée Svenko). Lucie, the second sister, had a degree in English. Around the age of 85, she developed a passion for modern mathematics and acquired a solid reputation in that field. I knew her well and remember that she had a horror of the colour blue. Hélène, the third sister, died young, in a mountain accident, when she had got no further than the baccalaureat. Louise, my grandmother, was fourth in line; she had progressed no further than an upper diploma but possessed a quite remarkable memory that allowed her, at a very advanced age, to name all the 454 sub-prefectures of France, and to position each one correctly on a map. Emma, her younger and last sister, acquired no diploma at all but was probably the most cultured and sophisticated of the five sisters. I was very fond of her; she was like a second grandmother to me. Apart from Hélène, all the sisters lived to ages of between 96 and 100.

In the spring of 1953, Aline made her last-but-one visit to Europe, to see her younger sisters and their families. She crossed the Atlantic on the *Queen Mary* and brought in her luggage numerous American presents. One was for me: a propelling pencil with four leads of different colours, an object then unknown in France. My cousin Catherine received one too. We were both 6 years old and were enchanted by such a present. Never had we held in our hands such a prodigious instrument. It was almost a magic wand. Its body of silvery metal bore four grooves into which a button made it possible to propel the lead of one's choice: red, blue, green or black. In response simply to pressure on the button, the lead returned into the body of the pencil. In Los Angeles the object must have cost just a few dollars; but in Paris it was priceless. And this object belonged to us, not to our parents: our delight was boundless. We played with our pens for months, even though we were slightly disappointed to learn that our cousins Pierre and Laurent had each received the same present.

I was the first to ruin my pencil. The leads were, it is true, fragile, and the propelling mechanism even more so. But Catherine kept hers for several years, although not long enough to switch immediately to the earliest ballpoint pens with four colours, luxury objects that were produced by the Jif-Waterman company and made their appearance in Europe in the early 1960s. These never seemed to me to possess the same attraction or the same perfections as the object that I had been given in 1953. Nor have I ever since come across any instrument so delectable to use for writing or colouring.

This magical object was my first tangible contact with the American world. Although it probably played an important role in my attraction to colours, it failed to attract me to America. I visited the United States for the first time a quarter of a century later and do not remember the trip with much pleasure. It was the month of December and freezingly cold. My first action upon arrival at Kennedy Airport was to purchase a woolly cap of a very nasty shade of red. It was not a good start. What surprised me most in this country that I believed to be ultra-modern, both on this trip and on all subsequent ones, was the rudimentary nature or even non-existence of signs, not only in towns but also on roads and motorways and in hotels, parking-lots, shopping centres and airports. There were very few signs, no direction indications and no system of orientation by means of a colour code. It was impossible to find one's way or move in the right direction without asking for help. It was nothing like old Western Europe in which one can travel in any direction without losing one's way, even if one is timid or not good at living languages. Codes, signs and colours of every kind guide a traveller from the very hearts of towns all the way to the depths of the countryside. Given that I belong to that class of shy and unchatty travellers, what I say is: long live old Europe!

SUNBATHING THROUGH THE YEARS

As a child I used to spend the long summer vacation in a seaside resort on the north coast of Brittany: Le Val-André. The beach, which was one of the finest in Western France, seemed immense to me and con-stituted a vast and inexhaustible playground for my friends and myself. There was no danger anywhere and we were allowed to do whatever we liked, whether on the beach, in the water or on the rocks. However, one activity that most of the children were allowed to engage in for as long as they liked was forbidden to two of us: those two were not allowed to lie on a towel and timidly acquire a sun-tan. Their grandmother, a stern woman always clad in grey, considered that to do so was dangerous, ridiculous and even (I perfectly recall the expression she used) 'of an insane vulgarity'. For her, sunbathing was an abomination. Not just the possession of a sun-tan but, even more, the acquiring of it. Adjectives would fail her when it came to qualifying this grotesque, degrading, obscene and immoral activity.

As I grew older, I realized that, contrary to what I had long believed, the opinion of this intransigent grandmother was shared by others, not all of them elderly, and even that, as the years passed, in our corner of the beach, at the foot of the Piégu cliff, the number of opponents to sunbathing was increasing. Several of my playmates who used to be free to lie motionless in the sunshine now no longer were. To be sure, good taste required that we did not remain as white as aspirins (at this time, in Brittany, the expression used was 'as white as cotton-wool'), but now it was enough to be just lightly tanned. Why this change in behaviour, on this beach, between the mid-fifties and the early sixties? Were people here better and earlier informed of the dangers of exposure to the sun? Did our little community include a few enlightened doctors who, well before the press took up the cry, had already pointed out the risks that one ran by doing too much sunbathing? No, not at all! The problem was one not of health but of social *mores*, social class, even snobbishness. But this was something that I did not realize until later, at the end of my adolescence, when I noticed that this part of the beach was frequented only by well-to-do families, while more modest ones, devoted to sunbathing, occupied the other end. Later still, much later, when, having become a historian, I began to take an interest in the history of colours, I discovered that what had happened on that beach of my childhood did not constitute an isolated case but, on the contrary, stemmed from a more general and long-standing phenomenon. Repeatedly, down through the decades and the centuries, there have been changes in polite society's attitude to the sun, the outdoors and skin-colours.

At this point, let us consider a little history.

Under the Ancien Régime and in the first half of the nineteenth century, still, in not only France but the whole of Western Europe, those who belonged to the aristocracy or the bourgeoisie felt obliged to have the palest and smoothest skin possible, in order to distinguish themselves from the peasants. The skin of the latter, who worked outdoors in the sun, was copper-coloured or rubicund and, in some cases, mottled with blotches: terrible! The possession of smooth, white skin and 'blue blood', that is to say veins visible beneath one's pale, almost transparent skin, was a 'must'. But in the second half of the nineteenth century, values changed. When 'polite society' took to frequenting the seaside and then, a little later, also the mountains, good taste dictated the display of a sun-tanned complexion and skin darkened by the rays of the sun. It was a matter of distinguishing oneself no longer from the peasants imprisoned in the countryside, but from the increasingly numerous workers; these lived in towns, worked indoors and so had white skin, a wan complexion and pale or greyish faces: appalling! It was above all imperative not to look like a worker, a creature far worse than a simple peasant. These new values and the quest for the sunshine that accompanied them increased in strength as the decades passed. They seem to have peaked between 1920 and 1960: the period when sunbathing was fashionable and one *had* to have a tan.

However, this did not last. From the mid-sixties onward, when seaside holidays and winter sports spread to the middle and even lower classes, that same 'polite society' progressively turned its back on sunbathing because it had become within the means of everyone, or almost everyone. Those on 'paid holidays', in particular, strove hard to acquire a tan: so distasteful, if not positively grotesque! What was truly chic now was *not* to have a tan, particularly if one had just returned from the seaside. Later, this attitude, which had started as a scornful snobbishness, gradually gained ground. But this time it was for reasons of health. The increase in cases of skin-cancer and illness caused by prolonged exposure to the sun caused sunbathing to lose ground, mainly among the middle classes. The possession of a suntan was no longer valued – quite the contrary. The balance has tilted in the opposite direction, as it often has in the history of value-systems. But for how long?

Today only social upstarts, starlets and a few 'celebrities' continue to sunbathe. But they hardly ever do so on a beach, lying in the sun. Instead, they lie in a studio, motionless beneath an artificial sun-lamp. This is obviously pretty ridiculous, even – to quote the grandmother of my two playmates – 'immoral and of an insane vulgarity'.

THE 'BLING' OF THE 1950s

What prompted my aversion to gold and gilt and, more generally, to all shiny colours? No doubt my childhood. In my family, gold figured neither in the objects of daily life nor in the household furnishings, nor in jewellery and clothing accessories. Obviously, the men in our family did not wear any jewellery and the women certainly avoided 'clinking' jewellery. Not that my parents and aunts and uncles were too poor for that. Rather, jewellery had nothing to do with the family *mores* and value-systems. In any case, in my family, to attach too much importance to one's appearance, clothing, décor and accessories was considered indecent and vulgar, even ridiculous. When I became a young man, then an adult, I could have rejected such behaviour and deliberately reacted against it. But that never happened. Like my parents and my uncles and aunts, I have remained indifferent to clothes and never carry any accessory about my body, not even a watch; and I feel affronted by anything that is shiny or eye-catching. Gold, in particular, disgusts me.

Searching through my childhood memories, I have found what may be an explanation for this repulsion which, with age, has become almost a phobia. Between the ages of 8 and 12, I was a Wolf-Cub. For as long as we lived up at the top of Montmartre, the pack to which I belonged geographically covered the borders of the 8th, 9th and 18th *arrondissements*. The great Salle des Pas Perdus of Saint-Lazare station was the place where we would gather and, later, disperse. On certain Sunday evenings, around six o'clock, after a scouting day devoted to a variety of activities (including humiliating and unproductive attempts to sell calendars), neither my father nor my mother was free to pick me up there. So I would go home with one of my older fellow-Cubs, who lived close to the Place Clichy. There, intimidated and ill at ease, I would wait to be rescued by my father and for our return to our house at the top of Montmartre, which was territory more familiar to me. The wait seemed interminable and the apartment where it took place was gloomy: too big, too meandering and too dark. The lighting, in particular, seemed far weaker than in our home, as if attempts were being made to economize. However, the most distressing thing was not the place itself but its owner: my fellow Wolf-Cub's grandmother, a severe widow, relatively young but seemingly not fond of children. She was constantly telling us off or ordering us about in a grating voice that still seems to resound in my ears. This acrimonious woman, always dressed in brown or black, was, in contrast, exaggeratedly highly made-up and was covered in jewellery: golden jewellery – or what I took to be so – round her neck, in her ears, on her arms, on her fingers and on her chest. She put me in mind of a wicked stepmother in a fairy-tale, or a king's second wife, who detested the children from his first marriage: Snow White's stepmother, for instance. Her jewellery sparkled and clinked. In short, it was the 'bling' of the 1950s and, even then, I found it unpleasant and disturbing.

My early rejection of gold was no doubt due to that woman and her anxiety-making apartment. Later on, it was confirmed through the influence of my uncle Henri, who was a second father to me. He was an austere Calvinist, a historian by profession, and would often assume the roles of pedagogue and head of our family. He liked to remind us that clothing is a sign of sin; in the earthly paradise, Adam and Eve were naked. They were ejected after eating the forbidden fruit and it was to mark that sin that they were given clothing. On that account alone, for my uncle and for most Protestant value-systems, trying to attract attention through one's clothing or its accessories, in particular jewellery, was behaviour unworthy of a good Christian or even an honest citizen: it was both vanity and an affront to others.

I was raised more or less with ideas such as these and, as a result, over the years, for me gold became a substance and a colour that I detested. And, perhaps even more than gold, which can sometimes be of a matt colour, I loathed gilt: in my eyes, this was the very embodiment of absolute vulgarity! To be sure, in this domain my own sensibility and sentiments are of no importance; they do not constitute historical documentation or even particularly remarkable evidence. All the same, contrary to what might be expected, quite a few people do perceive gold in this light.

In opinion polls conducted in order to discover the most liked and the most disliked colours, gold and silver are sometimes included among the colours and are referred to on a par with red, green, blue and so on. The polls show that, in Europe as a whole – where they have been conducted ever since the late nineteenth century – many of those questioned do not like gold. Here, though, we should take into account one major geographical difference: by and large, southern countries manifest a certain respect for gold, an attraction that is not shared by northern countries. Actually, this is a divide that is more cultural than strictly geographical. It is a matter not so much of luminosity, climate and the Mediterranean area, but rather of traditions and religion: gold is admired or tolerated in Catholic countries (as it is in Muslim ones), but it is more or less rejected in Protestant countries. Such geographical and cultural splits are accompanied by social ones. Contrary to one assumption, a fascination with gold is typical not of the aristocracy or the upper bourgeoisie, but of the minor bourgeoisie, social upstarts and, perhaps even more, the disadvantaged classes, for whom it retains a strong mythological dimension.

A BRIEF HISTORY OF GOLD

Writing the above lines, I realized that I was being unjust to those of my friends or, more simply, my contemporaries who do love gold, for its substance, and its luminosity. I was also being unjust to gold itself which, as a medieval historian, I have frequently encountered in my research work, and to which I have devoted various courses of study and lectures. Now I would like to do it justice by briefly noting a few features of its ancient history. There will be nothing anecdotal about this account and it will relate closely to colours.

This is a brilliant, luminous, malleable, untarnishable metal that is easy to extract and to work. It is present in a variety of forms throughout the world and seems always to have held fascination for human beings. In very early times it became a sign of power and wealth and performed many important economic functions. At the same time, it was surrounded by particular stories, at the heart of which the theme of a quest occupied a central place. Two stories from Greek mythology are exemplary in this respect: the quest for the golden apples of the gardens of the Hesperides, which was the eleventh labour of Heracles, and the tale of the golden fleece and Jason and his Argonauts' search for it. But Germanic mythology is not far behind, with its legend of the Nibelungen that revolves around the gold of the river Rhine and the search for and possession of it. Today, the pursuit of gold takes a different form: the heroes of our own day and age seek to win medals in the Olympic Games and other great championships. No other metal or material has stirred up such covetousness or engendered such a body of myths.

They originated long ago. The first seams of gold may not have been exploited before the fourth millennium BCE, but in all probability Paleolithic man had already noticed the presence in running water of metallic particles that could easily be gathered up in a handful of sand. Alongside shells and animals' teeth, these scraps and nuggets of fluvial or alluvial gold took their place in the first ornaments conceived by human beings. Later, in the Neolithic, that same gold inspired the creation of the most ancient metallic jewellery: rings, bracelets and necklaces. Thanks to its great malleability, it could be hammered and worked without being heated as other metals had to be. Furthermore, gold is resistant to fusion except at extremely high temperatures of 1,200 degrees or more.

Over and above its brilliance and colour, which were found attractive even in its native form, it was probably its material qualities – malleability, divisibility and the fact that it was easy to collect, extract, transport and manipulate – that, at an early date, conferred upon gold its superiority over other metals. Moreover, its (relative) rarity and its (remarkable) untarnishability encouraged the idea of storing it and using it as an intermediary in trading activities. As early as the second millennium BCE, in both Egypt and Mesopotamia, gold was being stored in the form of powder, nuggets, ingots, balls, leaves, rings, jewellery, table-ware and other precious objects. Gold coins made their appearance somewhat later: the first to be minted were Greek and date from only the seventh century BCE. By this time gold had already long since acquired an authentic fiduciary value and was playing an important economic role. Stamped ingots and disks were circulating throughout the Near and the Middle East and made it possible to introduce certain regulations; others provided reference values, particularly in Egypt which, in Antiquity, was the principal gold-producing power. By now gold was regarded not solely as merchandise, but also as a kind of measurement. Even if gold coins did not yet exist, the 'gold standard', for its part, was already firmly established 2,000 years before the birth of Christ – as, indeed, it still is today.

However, gold is ideal not only as a measure or a reserve-value. It can also circulate, be exchanged, passed from hand to hand. Gold can be touched, is dynamic, can be accepted and then returned, given and stolen, worked upon and transformed. It undoubtedly belongs to the world of metals and metallurgy – an underground, mysterious and dangerous world – but on its own it creates a world apart. The craftsman who worked on gold was not a blacksmith, an alarming figure who manipulated iron and fire; he was a goldsmith with a studio that, unlike a forge, in no way resembled some infernal cavern. A goldsmith was more than an artisan; he was an artist whose know-how was not merely technical but also aesthetic and learned. He was nothing like a sorcerer but was certainly full of enchantment, creating incomparable objects whose splendour and beauty had something magical about them. In the early Middle Ages, a goldsmith would be a monk, since gold-work was nearly always Church art. In modern times, he is a cultivated artist with many talents, who excels at working with all precious substances. In fact, for many years, goldsmiths were the intimate companions or advisers of kings and princes, following the example of the most famous of them, Saint Eloi (who died in 660), who was the bishop of Noyon and the 'minister' of the Merovingian kings, Clotaire and Dagobert.

An alchemist was quite different from a goldsmith. Like a black-smith, an alchemist transformed substances and possessed knowledge that was shrouded in secrecy. However, even if alchemy was the art of transmuting metals with a view to obtaining gold, that gold was more of a symbol or an allegory than a real substance to be attained. The alchemical process was based on a set of types of knowledge that were more hermetic and mystical than they were truly chemical: gold was not so much a precious metal as a metaphor for understanding, a spiritual asset or even a quest for the inaccessible. Symbolically, it was related to the sun, the source of life, warmth and light. Indeed, metal-lurgy and alchemy often associated stars with metals. The latter were regarded as the planets of the subterranean world – as it were, cosmic energies solidified and buried in the ground. Silver was often linked with the moon, but gold was always linked with the sun and possessed all the virtues of the latter.

All these qualities and properties of gold pose the problem of the hierarchy of materials and precious substances in different societies. Had gold always been placed in the top rank? It must be said that it had not. At times, silver and even copper were regarded as richer and more beneficial metals. But that was only in extremely ancient periods. By the second millennium BCE, in both the Egypt of the pharaohs and impe-rial China, gold was considered to be the first among metals, the per-fect metal, the most desired of all goods. In the West, in more recent times, competition came from another quarter, not from other metals but from precious stones. In the Middle Ages, in the treasuries of the Church and, still in the sixteenth and seventeenth centuries, in those of kings and princes, gold was overshadowed by gems. Emeralds, rubies, sapphires and, above all, diamonds were valued more highly. But in those days, what were admired more even than those gems were pearls. From the thirteenth century to the eighteenth, throughout Europe, pearls occupied the summit of the hierarchy. Gold came in third place – above all the other metals, to be sure, and above ivory and silk, ermine and sable, but below pearls and gem-stones.

However, gold is not just a substance: it is also light. For northern peoples, always seeking luminosity, this was its principal virtue: gold shines, illuminates, helps to emerge from the night and the shadows. It embodies a mineral brilliance, buried in the ground and to be brought into the light. Among the Celts and the German peoples, the quest for gold was often linked with a quest for light, as was the quest for the Holy Grail, so dear to medieval legends. The difference between those two quests was minimal: both gold and the Grail constituted divine lights, cosmic energies. The former was linked with the sun, the latter evoked the blood of Christ, both of them sources of life and light.

It was no doubt thanks to this luminous dimension, rather than to its rarity and price, that gold, right from ancient times, was associated with all that was sacred. From very early on, the temples of both the old and the new worlds assigned an important place to it, first as an offering to the gods, then as an essential element in the adornment of the temple and its cult. Gold, this brilliant metal and divine light, was an integral feature in the liturgy. In ancient temples and Christian churches alike, it helped to dissipate the shadows, creating an interplay of light and a sense of the presence of the divine. Its strong power of reflection sometimes assigned it the role of a mirror, making colours vibrate and filling the sacred space with an energy that mediated between earth and heaven.

This massive presence of gold in temples was the cause of plenty of controversies, as the Bible already records. There were many who, like the prophet Isaiah, regarded it as a kind of idolatrous cult that was offensive to God. With the advent of Christianity, this debate again came to the fore, first in the Romanesque period, then again at the beginning of modern times. Some prelates regarded gold as light, so considered that it should be abundantly present in churches since it helped to dissipate the darkness and spread the impact of the divine. One was Suger, the abbot of Saint-Denis, who, between 1130 and 1140, rebuilt and decorated the church of his abbey accordingly:

in it, objects of enamel and gold, illuminated books and the fabrics and vestments used all afforded gold a considerable presence. In the very same period, other prelates, such as the great Saint Bernard, the abbot of Clairvaux, believed, on the contrary, that gold was simply a substance, a vanity, a useless luxury that impeded contact with God: it should be avoided and banned from the sanctuary. This was a view that was drastically implemented in Cistercian churches. Later, in the sixteenth century, the great Protestant reformers adopted the views of Saint Bernard and urged that gold should be ejected from churches. According to Calvin, it was to be scorned, for it directed one away from the Truth and the Good. A few centuries later, however, the Catholic counter-reformation promoted the view that nothing was too beautiful for the house of God. This prompted a massive return of gold and colour, works of art and precious materials and vibrating light and sound effects. Baroque art turned churches into veritable theatres in which the place of gold was now all the more pervasive, given that the mines of the New World were providing the old Catholic Europe with hitherto inconceivable quantities of precious metals.

Was gold matter or light? The question had been hotly debated ever since ancient times and could really never be resolved, for gold was just as much light as it was matter. But there was more to it, for it was also colour. All the pictorial arts recognized this and integrated gold into their palettes, making it an element in its own right in their colour ranges. Gold was a colour. But what colour? As we see it nowadays, it is primarily associated with yellow. In children's pictures, common knowledge and ordinary symbolism and imaginary representations, gold is always a yellow metal. But this had not always been the case since, in the soil, even in its native state, the precious metal could display many different shades, ranging from white to red and passing by way of many yellows and oranges, pinks and beiges, browns and greys and even greens. Its natural range was extremely extensive.

At the cultural level, its range was more restricted. For a long time gold was associated with white more than with yellow, particularly among peoples that regarded it not so much as matter but as light. In ancient societies, light was white, not yellow, and gold represented a 'super-white', something beyond white. Such is the case, for example, in medieval illuminations: the gold backgrounds to miniatures, even if they look more or less yellow, are in no way related to that colour, which has a low standing in value-systems generally (since it is the colour of treachery and deceit). Those golden backgrounds, on the contrary, symbolize divine light, absolute clarity. When the painter placed colours on a golden background, for him it was as if he was placing them on a background that was whiter than white. Conversely, when the emphasis is on the materiality of gold, not on its luminosity, and more attention is being paid to its weight or power than to its purity and brilliance, it is associated with red. No ordinary red, of course, but a symbolic red that is dense, heavy, rich and imperial. This red-gold, omnipresent throughout the Mediterranean region, is a cousin of purple.

A MYSTERIOUS SHADE OF GREEN

When I was about 14 years old, I discovered a new shade of green, never seen before and, I think, never seen since. At any rate, my memory has not retained any trace of it. In truth, I never really saw this new shade of green (green has been my favourite colour ever since my earliest childhood) but had only read about it. It was in my *lycée*, shortly prior to the long summer holidays. The atmosphere was already summery and a number of lessons had been cancelled, so that the pupils of Year 4 were spending much of their time in recreation, under the lazy supervision of teaching assistants hardly older than they were. Tired of playing football with an old tennis ball, unwilling to open my schoolbooks, impatient to leave and with nothing to do, I set about reading the notice-board displaying 'official advice and information' – something that I never usually did. Some of the information was hard for me to understand, in particular that relating to the budget, questions to do with the school statutes and a new way of recruiting suppliers. However, I had no trouble at all in understanding a piece of information that directly concerned me, or at least the fifth-year classes and the next school year, which began in October.

The school authorities informed the pupils and their parents that, during the summer, in order to increase the number of classrooms, new buildings would be constructed in the park, providing eight new classrooms for the forthcoming school year. The word 'prefabricated' did not appear but any reader, even an adolescent such as myself, understood that these would be no more than simple huts. The text, which waxed on verbosely about security regulations, did also provide a little information as to the size and positioning of these buildings and, in particular, announced what colours they would be: the exteriors would be rendered in white and beige materials while, inside, the corridors and classrooms would, 'for the comfort of both pupils and teachers', be painted an 'administrative green'. An administrative green!

The expression delighted me and my school-mates and, even today, still makes me smile. What could an 'administrative green' possibly be? No-one knows, nor did anyone in 1961. Yet we can all imagine it without too much difficulty: a green on the light side rather than dark, verging on grey, already dirty-looking from the very start and that reflects all the melancholy of public functions: in other words, a relatively restricted range of colour. Thinking more about this, I realized that the expression is more evocative and possibly more precise than any informational code that refers to a colour chart: Pantone 341, Munsell GY 9.47 and so on. Unless one happens to be a professional working with colours, without such a chart actually before us, those figures tell us nothing at all. Whereas an 'administrative green' . . .

Words possess infinite chromatic powers. Any adjective associated with any colour term bestows upon it a particular nuance and sets it within a far more dream-like colour range than any colour chart produced by science or industry. Every one of us can thus try to create new colours, linking the imagination of a poet to the sensitivity of a painter. And we need not be limited to adjectives: proper and common nouns also have their virtues – a debonair blue, a Boniface red, a Sunday white, a mashed-potato yellow, the grey of a burglar's jemmy, a Saint-Pol-de Léon green, a Henri III pink, a Mitterrand beige (see above) . . .

One last word on the 'administrative green': at the Lycée Michelet in Vanves, the prefabricated buildings planned for the school year starting in 1961 were never constructed, so nobody, neither teachers nor pupils, was ever able to glory in the delicious wellbeing supposed to accompany that uncertain shade of green.

DO YOU SEE RED CLEARLY?

Few of us ever get the chance to test their colour vision. It seems to be of no interest to ophthalmologists, and even less to opticians. Only a handful of particular professions connected with the navy or with aviation, or even with research or forms of transport, insist on such a test when hiring someone. What exactly are they looking for? I do not know. It is true that I did, once in my life, undergo such a test, but it was carried out in such an improbable fashion that I can say nothing about either its methods or its aims.

It took place a few months before my departure for military service, in the course of the famous 'three-day' ritual that replaced the mythical old recruiting board. Like the latter, these three days were supposed to decide the selection, orientation and assignments of the future conscripts. It made a strong impression on the young men of my generation as, for many of them, this was their first contact with the military world, which was, to say the least, somewhat exotic.

After a hasty medical examination and a reading test designed to detect possible short-sightedness, an uncommissioned officer wearing shabby fatigues, installed in an improvised kind of hut resembling a voting booth, asked me if my colour-sight was good. 'Yes', I replied. He then repeated the question, to which I again responded in the affirmative. At this point he enquired, suspiciously, if I 'distinguished red clearly' from other colours. Again I said 'yes'. Then followed a dialogue worthy of Jarry or Courteline: 'Are you certain of that?', 'Yes', 'It's important, you know', 'I do know, but I have no difficulty in recognizing red', 'Fine, you may leave and tell the next man to come in.'

Of course, I did not understand what was going on at all, least of all the motives for this interrogation focused solely on red, and not on blue, green or yellow. Did the French army have a problem with this colour? When compounded with the fate reserved for red when the tricolour flag is furled, this grotesque interview in that ridiculous booth prompts one to wonder. Likewise, or even more, I could not understand why an examination concerning one's colour vision was limited to a brief conversation and dispensed with any visual exercises. There was no equipment indicating that any such exercise was envisaged. The fact was that not one of my comrades was asked to look at any colours, either in isolation or alongside other colours, or to name them. But they all underwent the same interrogation about red. Why red? Was it a matter of discovering evidence of colour-blindness? If that was the case, using words, not sight, to do so was a strange way of proceeding.

Ophthalmological medicine gives the name Daltonism to the visual condition that prevents one from distinguishing either all colours (achromatopsy) or, more commonly, two colours, one from another, in particular red and green or even certain reds and certain greens (dys-chromatopsy or Daltonism: colour-blindness in the strict sense). The English physicist and chemist, John Dalton (1766–1844), was one of the greatest scientists of all time and the true creator of atomic theory. He was the first to draw attention to this condition, from which he himself suffered. Today it is recognized that, in different forms, it affects 2 per cent of all men (but very few women). In most cases, it is congenital or hereditary and is rarely contracted. As far as we know today, it is caused by incomplete differentiation between the cones and rods of the retina, or else by imperfect connections with certain strands in the optic nerve. (The cones react to longer wave-lengths – reds, oranges; the rods to shorter ones – greens, blues). Colour-blindness is not a disease but a condition, which, although not at all grave, rules out exercising certain professions, principally those in which great use is made of coloured signals.

Historians have sometimes been perplexed when confronted by works devoted to colour-blindness or to other anomalies of colour-vision. They are, for example, surprised to find that John Dalton discovered his confusion of red and green at a moment – in the early nineteenth century – when, in Western culture, green was beginning to be regarded as the opposite of red, which had not been the case in the past. Meanwhile, anthropologists were wondering what 'normal' vision of colours really means and what 'anomalies in colour-vision' might be. They knew that the perception of colours is partly a neuro-biological phenomenon and partly a cultural one, which is why it varies in time and space and is not identical in all periods and all societies. They also knew that it is hard to apprehend colours without resorting to language – in other words, to culture: for the name of a colour is an integral part of it. So this notion of 'anomalies' seems questionable; the word 'differences' would suffice.

But what can we really know about such 'differences'? When two individuals find themselves in the same room, looking at the same object, and are asked to say what colour it is, even if they both reply 'blue', we cannot be sure that they see the same colour. Between the real colour, the perceived colour and the colour named (or represented), there exist countless networks of confusion, improvisation and contaminations.

Similarly, can one really explain to someone blind from birth what happens when we see colours? Can we make him feel what the notions of red, green and blue represent for a seeing person? Can one even communicate about such problems? Can a man who sees colours and one who has never seen them discuss them? Do they have compatible notions about colour-blindness? Does not the very asking of such questions, which many philosophers from Plato down to Wittgenstein have engaged in, underline the completely vain nature of all discourse about colour?

In this respect, the case of animals seems even more significant. What can we really know of animals' vision of colours? It is man himself who sets up experiments, provokes stimuli, observes how the animal in question behaves, and comments upon his own observations. All the tests, measurements, calculations and analytical and interpretative grids are established, coded and decoded by human beings. What can such people really tell us about animals? Not very much, except that different species do not react in the same way to the same stimuli; that bees seem excited by certain colours, bulls by others; that owls of all kinds seem able to distinguish many shades of grey, while rabbits dislike blue and pigs dislike pink. It is, indeed, not very much and, furthermore, it is all extremely questionable.

NO PURPLE FOR CHILDREN

The remarkable thing about colours is that they concern everyone, as I have often noticed when delivering public lectures. Whereas, on other subjects, the audience, when invited to speak once the lecturer has finished, sometimes remains dumb, intimidated or even uninterested and incapable of asking a single question, colour, on the contrary, loosens all tongues and the lecturer finds himself obliged to reply to a torrent of questions and remarks, especially when the audience contains the inevitable amateur psychologists or seekers of archetypes who are partial to esotericism. On a subject such as colour, such people turn out to be unstoppable.

Children are no exception. Colour similarly unlocks their tongues and sets them talking. I have several times been invited to speak in primary schools and so have had a chance to notice how colours – like animals – easily capture the interest of the very youngest – in fact, passionately engage them. With no hesitation, they named their favourite colours, mocked those that they did not like, associated one particular colour with a particular idea, another with an emotion or feeling. The symbolism of colours seemed to hold no secrets for them. Getting children to talk is always instructive for a specialist, and a joy for everyone.

A few years ago I was invited to speak about colours in a primary school in the Marais quarter of Paris. It was a CMI class (intermediate course, first year) and its pupils were aged between 8 and 10. In preparation for my visit, their teacher had decided to organize various instructive games and to divide the class into five teams: blues, reds, yellows, greens and purples. She asked the children, both boys and girls, to line up in one of these teams and tried to see that all the teams were roughly the same size. This proved impossible: no pupil wanted to be in the purple team – not one, out of 27 or 28. Of course we tried to find out why. Several of them declared that purple 'was not a colour for children'. By this they meant that it was a colour for 'old people'. One child even explained that a friend of her grandmother had 'purple hair'; another said that every year she gave her grandparents purple soap as a Christmas present. Others, more numerous, stressed that, for them, purple was not on a par with blue, red, yellow and green. For that reason alone, membership of the purple team would be demeaning. The latter observation is particularly interesting to a historian of colours. It suggests that, for children, green and purple, two colours claimed to be 'complementary' ones, should not be classified in the same category. Green has the same status as blue, red and yellow, but purple does not. By passing such a judgement, children show that they are perfectly aware of social and cultural practices that classify the colour green on the same level as the other three. But they are far less aware of scholarly classifications, taught (unfortunately) as early as the preparatory class, which present green as a composite colour, a half-colour, a second-rank colour, along with purple and orange. Chemists and physicists should lend an ear to children and revise their chromatic taxonomies!

One pupil stood out in this class that was hostile to purple. To be sure, like the others, he did not want to be in the purple team, particularly if he would be on his own there, but he refused to give his reasons. He declared that they were 'secret'. The class-teacher and myself were prepared to leave him with his secret, but his classmates soon set about discovering it. Mockery, jibes and assurances eventually got the timid lad (who was actually not really that timid) to crack and he quietly declared, 'Purple brings bad luck.' Far from laughing or disagreeing, most of the other children agreed with him: yes, purple does bring bad luck.

The history of this colour seems to bear out their opinion, partially at least. It is worth briefly considering it.

For ourselves, today, purple is a mixture of blue and red; to us, this seems self-evident, if not a positive truth. But for ancient societies that knew nothing of the spectrum and that classified colours differently, that was not the case. Purple had hardly anything to do with red and very little to do with blue. It was simply a particular type of black. Furthermore, in medieval Latin, one of the words commonly used to describe purple was *subniger*, 'sub-black' or 'half-black'. The Catholic system of liturgical colours has prolonged this ancient concept of purple right down to the present day: like black, purple is a colour of affliction and penitence; purple is for Advent and Lent, black is for Good Friday; purple for semi-mourning, black for full mourning. The Christian purple certainly seems to be a substitute for black.

At the end of the Middle Ages, however, ordinary purple was treated to a change of status. Although it still bore no relation to red, on the axis of colours it now found a place in between blue and black. In pictures, purple was no longer regarded as a particular type of black, for it could also take on a bluish tinge, especially a dark blue one. It was not a colour much liked as it was considered false and changeable. Chemically, it was unstable, both as a dye and as a paint. That is why, symbolically, purple – along with yellow – represents false and perfidious beings, starting with Ganelon, the traitor in the *Chanson de Roland*. In truth though, in the twelfth-century text, nothing associates that figure with this colour. Nevertheless, in the fifteenth and sixteenth centuries, the expression 'Ganelon's purple' is quite commonly used to describe the colour of treachery.

Later, in the second half of the seventeenth century, when Newton carried out his experiments with the prism and revealed the spectrum – that is to say, a new order for colours – purple finally slotted into place in-between red and blue. Now its symbolism was reassessed. By the nineteenth century it became the emblematic colour of bishops (cardinals having long since been assigned red) and for the first time it attracted the attention of artists and poets. The Symbolists, in particular, regarded it as a 'secret' colour, associated with the mysterious side of beings and things.

Today, for many of our contemporaries, purple is considered and perceived as being closer to red than to blue. But it is still disliked. It is always cited in first or second place when people are asked to name the colours that they do not like. Only brown seems even more unpopular. For most Europeans, purple is aggressive, eccentric, disturbing. Some women, like the children mentioned above, even believe that it brings bad luck: not for anything in the world would they dress in purple. On the contrary, though, designers, stylists and creative figures seeking change or to be provocative regard it as a 'subtle, inventive colour, full of meaning'. Some even predict that it will become 'the colour of the twenty-first century', no less!

THE WHIMS OF MEMORY

In some situations, the imagination stimulates the memory, accompanying it in its meandering and jolts and helping it to seek within itself some recollection buried beneath several layers of daily realities that are inevitably trivial and burdensome. But there are other cases, probably more numerous, in which one's memory and one's imagination follow opposed paths, entering into conflict as each struggles to impose its own feelings about the past.

As a traveller, I am very familiar with these clashes between my memory and my imagination. When preparing to set off to discover some town, region or country never visited before, in the weeks or months leading up to my departure, I progressively construct a certain image of the place, an image that is vague at first but becomes increasingly clear. I do so on the basis of my reading, photographs and the accounts of friends, relatives and colleagues. What could be more natural? But I also draw on proper names that designate that particular town or region or that are associated with it. For me, as for many others, including the narrator of *À la recherche du temps perdu*, place-names are strongly evocative, particularly where colours are concerned. Frequently, a particular sonority, spelling, rhythm or distribution of vowels helps to conjure up real colours (my colours) for a mental image that neither texts nor photographs had been able to determine in a definitive manner. In the case of a projected voyage, this colouring suggested by names increases the sense of happiness – what the German language excellently calls *Vorfreude* (anticipatory pleasure) – that precedes any departure for new horizons. Here, as in other circumstances, joy consists in an expectation of joy.

Then comes the voyage, with all its discoveries, ups-and-downs and encounters. Once I have reached my destination, I realize that the image of this town or country that I have created for myself is not correct with regard to either forms and topography, atmosphere and population, or colours and the general feeling that these produce. It would all have to be corrected to a greater or lesser degree and I was happy to do so, sometimes mocking myself for having tried to be 'a little Proust' and for having, yet again, been the victim of my imagination and naive enough to believe that the name of a town rich in 'a's, for example, necessarily implied an abundant presence of tiles or bricks. It had all been a matter of facile poetry, conventional painting, trumpery word-play and trashy assonances. Of course it had.

But then it was time to return. Little by little, the exact image of the town or country, corrected in the very places that I had visited, and fixed by postcards and photographs, became less clear, faded and changed. After a few weeks or months, another image returned and became fixed in my memory: the image that I had fabricated before setting out and which, in many cases, was very different from what I had seen on the spot, particularly with regard to colours. And this was the image that could not be effaced. In that case, what is the point of travelling? I know that it is this first image, the only 'true' one, rich in all the colours of the imaginary representation, that I shall retain until the end of my days. It is as if, for me, the recollection of what I dreamed up was more powerful than the memory of what I had lived through. For a poet, such an experience is not unusual; in fact it is frequent, and essential, as the whole of Nerval's poetry admirably illustrates. But in the case of a historian . . .?

PREFERENCES AND OPINION POLLS

Only once, when I was in my fifties, have I been accosted in the street for the purposes of an opinion poll on colour. It was quite late in the evening, on the day before Christmas Eve, in Paris, on the Boulevard Haussman, not far from the major Printemps department store. A sad-looking young woman, clad in an even sadder brown coat, asked me what my favourite colour was. 'Green', I replied, as I would have done thirty or forty years earlier if asked such a question, and as I still would today. I have always liked green, both in general and for some of its particular shades, especially its darker ones and those that verge on grey. My preference has nothing to do with the fashion for ecology.

My reply had been brief and rapid, but the young woman took several minutes to fill in countless papers and tick a number of different boxes. She did not enquire about my geographical origins or my professional activities, but she did ask me if I was 'over sixty'. This vexed me somewhat, as I was ten years younger. It is true that she was, herself, about twenty and I must have seemed positively senile to her. At that time I had already published several books and articles on the history of colours and had several times commented on the results of opinion polls on favourite and most disliked colours. So I tried to engage her in conversation and learn more about the agenda and the aims of the enquiry in which she was engaged, wishing to show that I too was a specialist on the matter. In vain. Without a word, she turned her back on me and moved off into the crowd. She had probably taken me for a more or less tipsy mentally deficient individual, or even for a tout seeking an opportunity to sell her drugs. When one is fat and bald and red-faced as well, it is not easy to engage in conversation with an unknown woman without arousing scorn or suspicion.

For a historian, the most important information provided by such opinion polls on favourite colours probably lies in the fact that the results have always been the same, ever since such enquiries began – that is to say, since the late nineteenth century. They appeared first in Germany in the years between 1880 and 1890; then, around 1900, in the United States; and after World War I they spread throughout the Western world. Marketing and publicity businesses, although still in their infancy, were already commissioning such polls. Down through the following decades, the method adopted to conduct this kind of enquiry has changed hardly at all. It consists in questioning people in the street, asking them, quite simply, 'What is your favourite colour?' To be valid and taken into account, the response must be clear and spontaneous: one straightforward colour-term, not two or three, nor qualified by a term indicating a particular shade, let alone accompanied by quibbling or cavilling seeking to establish whether the question concerns clothing, furnishings, painting, etc. No, this is a simple and direct question and it must be answered simply and directly. What is at stake is not how the colour comes to be used, not its material appearance; it is its imaginary representation.

In Europe, that imaginary representation has changed not at all. Despite all the accompanying changes in societies and sensibilities, new types of technology, new methods of illumination, and new materials that are coloured, the poll results hardly vary at all from one generation to the next. Whether one is in 1890, 1930, 1970 or 2000, blue always comes top of the list (in between 40 and 50 per cent of responses); next comes green (around 15 to 20 per cent); red is a little lower (around 12 to 15 per cent); white and black are left far behind (around 5 to 8 per cent for each); yellow, disliked by many, comes in last place with less than 2 per cent. 'Second-rank' colours (pink, orange, grey, purple and brown) are left to share no more than crumbs from the table.

Not only do results not vary from one decade to another, but they are more or less the same in all European countries, across the board from Portugal to Poland and from Greece to Norway. Neither climate nor history nor religion nor cultural traditions, let alone political regimes or levels of economic development, seem to impact upon favourite and disliked colours. Everywhere blue comes in first place, above green and red, and yellow brings up the rear. More surprising still: this classification of favourite colours is the same for men and for women, for all age-groups and for all socio-professional categories. Only young children diverge somewhat from this pattern, giving red a higher place – almost on a level with blue – and giving yellow a slightly higher place, being less disliked than by adults.

Those are the results for Europe and they differ hardly at all for other countries that belong to the Western world: the United States, Canada, Australia and New Zealand. But elsewhere the results are different. In Japan, for instance, white comes in first place, followed by red and pink; in China red is ahead of both yellow and blue. In India and the Indo-Chinese peninsula, pink and orange are held in higher esteem than in Europe, while blue, for its part, is not much liked. As for the peoples of black Africa and Central Asia, they sometimes find it hard to adapt to colour parameters as defined by Western culture (in terms of hue, luminosity and saturation). Faced with any given tint, it may be more important to know whether it is dry or wet, soft or hard, smooth or uneven, than to decide whether it belongs to the range of reds, blues or yellows. Colour is not really anything in itself, and is even less a phenomenon associated solely with sight. It is apprehended in the same manner as other sensory parameters so, in that case, 'European-type' enquiries into notions of favourite or disliked colours are pretty meaningless.

These differences between societies are fundamental, for they emphasize the almost exclusively cultural character of everything to do with colour. They reveal the relative nature of what Western science claims to be truths (the spectrum, the chromatic circle, primary colours and complementary ones, the law of simultaneous contrasts, etc.) and they prompt greater prudence in the domain of comparative studies. It behoves historians and sociologists, as well as ethnologists, to bear this in mind.

7

WORDS

BROWN AND BEIGE

Some stages in learning to deal with a lexicon are more decisive than others. In the domain of colours it seems to me that, in French, the switch from *marron* (chestnut) to *brun* (brown) constitutes one of these stages, as one emerges from childhood. Young French speakers are often unaware of the term *brun* and when they begin to use it, it is applied solely to hair. Not many of them at this point connect it with *marron* or realize that the two terms are synonymous. *Brun*, as an adjective, figures hardly at all in the language of childhood. It is usually a proper noun, the name of a bear or of a series of bears, the successors to Brun, the clumsy hero of *Le Roman de Renart*. These have been extremely common in children's books for almost a century.

Marron (literally 'chestnut' in English), on the other hand, is a word often used by young French children. For them, it covers an extremely extensive chromatic field ranging from red ochre to almost black, but it is hardly ever divided into different shades, unlike red or blue, which children differentiate clearly by the time they are 5 or 6 years old. They like using the word *marron*, which they associate with the round conkers that they use in their games and also with a more or less scatological colour. *Marron* is not a rude word but it often provokes laughter. Later, around the age of ten or eleven, when they have grown up a bit and possess a richer colour vocabulary, the term *marron*, in certain of its uses at any rate, begins to fall away before the advance of *brun*. By the time adolescence is reached, a continued use of *marron* in every context and for all shades of the colour is in many cases a sign of immaturity or retarded language skills. Later still, in adulthood, a continued preference for *marron* rather than *brun*, when speaking, is characteristic of men or women who have never become aware of lexical subtleties. Anyone attentive to language will, on the contrary, make use of both words, introducing nuances of meaning and colouration to distinguish them.

While *brun* is relatively neutral or polyvalent, which ultimately comes to the same thing, *marron* is more evocative of the reddish aspects of the colour, analogous to those of the chestnuts that bear the same name. But it also expresses the idea of a warm, wet brown that may bring excrement to mind. Hence the pejorative connotation that this word may acquire when it designates a particular shade of brown. Moreover, the origin of the word is obscure. The adjective, in common use in the eighteenth century, is certainly derived from the name given to chestnuts, but this noun, which itself appeared in botanical terminology in the early 1500s, has no known etymology.

The case of the word *beige*, the etymology of which is equally uncertain and controversial, is at once similar and also different. Although it is attested in the thirteenth century, when it described natural wool that was neither dyed nor bleached, the adjective only became widely used in the course of the nineteenth and twentieth centuries. Moreover, until recent times, it seems not to have affected all age-groups or all social circles. It is a word with which most young children are unfamiliar, or that they use without really knowing to what shade it corresponds. You have to be quite mature to use it correctly. Besides, it is not in general usage. I recollect that, forty or so years ago, in the rural areas of Western France (Brittany, Normandy and Maine), *beige* was a term that was practically unknown. Everything that would elsewhere have been described by this word (shoes, bags, clothing) was simply called 'yellow' – possibly with a hint of scorn since this dull, rather dirty yellow was a product of city-living and was accordingly regarded as eccentric, if not positively vulgar. In the countryside of lower Normandy, for example, 'yellow' (*beige*) shoes were contrasted to 'black' (that is, dark) shoes and to red (that is, mahogany or wine-coloured) shoes. In 1872, Littré was already noting that 'in some provinces, "yellow linen" is the expression used for linen that is untreated and with a beige tinge'.

Nowadays though, *beige* is in common use and has even been the subject of a remarkable promotion in the hierarchy of colours. Beige, which used to be no more than a shade, has now been recognized as a colour in its own right, not only in the fashion world but also in a number of other domains of daily life – not as a colour of the first rank, of course, as are red, blue, green and yellow, but as a secondary colour, as are pink and purple. The most surprising thing about this promotion is that it is due not to truly chromatic considerations ... but to number symbolism. If, as I have emphasized repeatedly in the course of this book, one distinguishes six 'basic' colours (white, red, black, green, yellow and blue) and five second-rank colours (purple, orange, pink, grey and brown) – all the rest being mere nuances or nuances of nuances – one obtains a total of eleven colours. Eleven: nothing symbolic about that number! It suggests either an excess (ten plus one) or a lack (twelve minus one). At a social or a cultural level, it is not possible to set colours in order starting with such a number. It was therefore necessary to find a twelfth colour (for twelve is a totality, a kind of perfection), which meant promoting what was no more than a nuance to the rank of a colour. Over the past few decades, Western societies have chosen beige for this purpose. In this way a balance is restored: there are now six basic colours and six second-rank ones.

We should congratulate beige on this remarkable promotion. It testifies to the fact that although, in the world of colours (in so far as they are concepts), genuine changes are rare and slow, they nevertheless are possible.

SPELLING AND GRAMMAR

The plans for reforming the spelling of the French language make my hair stand on end. Not only because they consider writing solely in its utilitarian function, forgetting that it also constitutes an aesthetic, a poetics, an invitation to dream; but above all because they are based on a postulate that seems to me questionable. This is that spelling is difficult to learn, too difficult for the young of today. Is that true? In primary school, in college and at the *lycée*, a pupil acquires an understanding of subjects far more arduous than spelling: physics, for example, which is undeniably complex and stems from concepts and reasoning that it is hard for most ordinary mortals to grasp. I humbly admit that, throughout my schooldays, I understood – so to speak – nothing in that discipline (nor was I alone in that respect), while spelling, on the contrary, presented no problem at all. And what can be said of computing? Ministers, educationalists and the media sometimes speak of 'those whom spelling has left behind, handicapped in their studies and then in their daily lives and in their search for employment'. But what about those whom information technology has left behind? They are far more numerous and, these days, far more handicapped too. Who is bothered? Nobody, for most of them are men and women in the third or fourth stages of life, electors and economic agents who will soon have disappeared.

That being said, it is only fair to recognize that the subtleties and inconsistencies of French spelling are legion, as indeed are those of grammar. Why is an *s* needed in *inclus* (included) but not in *exclu* (excluded)? Why is there no elision in expressions such as *le onzième siècle* or *la messe de onze heures*? Why is a singular verb used in a phrase such as *plus d'un est venu* (more than one has come)? The dialectics of correct usage and the logic of meaning do not always coincide. Language is not a code and writing is not a machine – and for this we should rejoice, for if that were the case most of the humanities would not exist.

Where grammar and spelling are concerned, it is perhaps in the agreement of adjectives of colour that the rules of correct usage are the hardest to assimilate. There are hardly any problems in the case of ordinary adjectives, constructed from basic terms: 'une robe verte' (a green dress), 'une chemise blanche' (a white shirt), 'des yeux bleus' (blue eyes). But it becomes more complicated when the colour adjective is represented by a noun or is completed by another adjective. In principle, the names of plants or minerals used as terms of colour remain invariable (i.e., do not, in French, vary in gender or number), except where this adjectival use is longstanding and frequent. But who decides on its age and frequency? Thus, words such as *rose* (pink), *violet* (purple) or even *cramoisi* (crimson) agree in number and gender with the noun that they qualify, as any adjective would: 'des joues roses' (pink cheeks), 'des rubans violets' (purple ribbons), 'des étoffes cramoisies' (crimson fabrics); but for some words, introduced into colour vocabulary more recently, the rule is sometimes unclear. While terms such as *crème*, *ivoire*, *paille* and *jade* (cream, ivory, straw-coloured and jade) nearly always remain invariable, others, such as *orange, cerise, pourpre, émeraude, incarnat* (orange, cherry, crimson-purple, emerald, incarnadine – i.e., red) agree or do not agree depending on the author who is using them: 'des robes pourpre(s)' (purple dresses), 'des foulards orange(s)' (orange head-scarves), 'des lèvres incarnat(es)' (red lips), 'une longue chevelure châtain(e)' (long, chestnut-coloured hair). Some terms go as far as agreeing in number but not in gender. So one would not say 'des vaches marrones' (brown cows) but one *would* write 'des esclaves marrons' (maroons), for here the meaning of *marrons* does not refer directly to the colour. Sometimes, even – and this is supremely illogical – one finds 'des chaussures marrons' (brown shoes): the noun is feminine but the adjective is masculine. This is a spelling that is condemned by some purists but accepted by others. As for composite adjectives, they are usually invariable so as not to break the semantic unity that they constitute: 'des chemises bleu clair' (pale blue shirts), 'des écharpes rouge vif' (bright red scarves), 'des tapis vert olive' (olive-green mats), 'des chaussettes gris-bleu' (blue-grey socks); but there are a number of exceptions to this rule, such as 'des teintures rouges (plural) et or (singular)' (red-and-gold draperies) or 'des robes pie-noires' (black-and-white dresses).

Far from being anecdotal, these hesitations concerning spelling and grammar underline the extent to which colour-terms are distinctive categories, for they include not only adjectives and nouns but also much more. Lexical specialists should surely recognize this: they are words that are grammatically difficult to classify and semantically hard to control. Their evocative power, their free associations and their rebellious nature make them terms that are far too strong not only to obey the rules of grammar but also to be confined to a single level of meaning. Faced with a short sentence such as the following: 'The young woman entered the room wearing a white shirt and a red skirt', who could naively believe that the words *red* and *white* simply designate the colours of the clothes? Who? And as for the story of Little Red Ridinghood or that of Bluebeard, well . . .

A DAY AT THE RACES

I have never felt attracted to horses and even less so to horse races. As for the turf system of bets of 3 to 1, 4 to 1 or 5 to 1, this makes me uneasy, and, like all gaming involving money, I consider it immoral. Nevertheless, when I was about twenty years old, one of my close friends discovered the joys and hopes of betting on three horses at a time. For several weeks, on Sunday mornings, I queued up with him at a tobacconist's in the 17th *arrondissement*, where one could bet on the afternoon's races. I did not myself place any bets. But I did observe the unknown world of gamblers in which the social classes intermingled and a vocabulary unknown to me was used. The terms for the colours of the horses' coats fascinated me: bay, roan, skewbald, dun . . . In them, as in the colours of a coat of arms, I detected a mysterious music and poetry.

A little later, my friend took the next step and began to frequent the Vincennes race course. Once, just once, I accompanied him. I recollect that it was cold and misty and that ordinary spectators could make out very little in the various races. And I also remember having again heard several of the people around me pronouncing these strange terms used to describe the colours of horses' coats. I decided to find out more and, for several weeks, with the help of my cousin Catherine – who had been attracted to horses ever since her early years – and also that of various books that I consulted in the library, I acquired in this domain an expertise that allowed me to adopt a quite pedantic role among my family and friends. I was not yet a historian of colours but everything about them interested me. Today, I have forgotten some of the subtleties of this horse-racing vocabulary, but many terms do remain in my memory. Actually, quite a few of them are already to be found in the medieval *chansons de geste* and tales of chivalry. To be familiar with them is quite useful to a medievalist.

Contrary to what might be believed, this lexicon, sometimes considered pedantic, if not ridiculous, is neither very rigorous nor particularly scientific. Like everything pertaining to colour, it is based on subjective impressions and classifications and shares more in common with the palette of a painter or a poet than with that of a zoologist. Furthermore, mixing, as it does, ancient, almost obsolescent, terms with words that belong to everyday language, but with their meanings somewhat distorted, it seems to delight in creating uncertainties and confusions. It is as if the primary function of this lexicon was not so much to describe the colour of a horse's coat as to exclude the non-initiated from the micro-world that uses this language. Similar lexical strategies, more ideological than strictly semantic, exist in all domains of knowledge and in all social circles. Linguists must certainly be familiar with them.

Let me now cite a few of these unusual terms and thereby confirm that every lexicon is first and foremost a poetics.

The word *robe* (coat) designates the hairs and the mane of a horse. This coat, which is darker at birth than in adulthood, may vary with the seasons, being paler in the summer, darker in the winter. It may be monochrome, or polychrome. If a horse has a coat of a single colour it may be *blanc* (white) (a theoretical notion since, in almost all cases, it is in fact a very pale grey), *noir* (black), *gris* (grey) or *alezan* (chestnut). That last word does not refer to a precise colour but to all single-colour coats that fall between pale *fauve* (tawny) and dark brown. A precise adjective sometimes specifies such a chestnut coat: *claire* (pale), *brulée* (burnt), *dorée* (golden). If the horse possesses a composite coat, terms may vary. If the body is one colour while the limbs, mane and tail are black, the horse may be a *bai* (bay) (if the body is reddish-brown), an *isabelle* (dun) (with a yellowish or milky-coffee-coloured body), or else *souris* (mousey) (with an ash-grey body). If the body, limbs and mane are composed of two intermingling colours, the horse may be *aubère* (red roan) (with white and reddish hairs), *louvet* (wolf-coloured) (with reddish and black hairs) or *gris* (grey). That word *gris* (grey), which may be completed by an assortment of nuancing terms (*gris-fer* (iron-grey), *gris-tourdille* (dull-grey), etc., refers sometimes to a monochrome coat, sometimes to a two-tone one. When a red roan horse has a coat on the pale side, it is called *fleur de pêcher* (peach blossom) or *pêchard* (peachy); if the coat is darker, it is known as *fleur de lilas* (lilac blossom). If the coat is composed of three colours (in many cases, two for the body and one for the extremities), the horse is called roan. If the coat has patches of two colours, one of them being white, the horse is described as *pie* (piebald), *pie alezan* (chestnut piebald), *pie noir* (black piebald) or *pie bai* (bay piebald), if the colour white dominates; but if white does not dominate, it is described as *alezan pie*, *noir pie* or *bai pie*. Finally, a horse with a multi-coloured coat with irregular stripes or blotches is called, depending on its colouring: *tigré* (striped), *moucheté* (dappled), *bordé* (fringed), *truité* (speckled), *hermine* (ermine), *pommelé* (mottled), *moiré* (moiré), *neigé* (snowy) or even *rouanné* (roanish) or *auberisé* (red roanish).

This French lexicon, which is complex to study philologically, was not codified until 1937, in the *Traité d'hippologie* produced by the Saumur Cavalry School. But it is not so much practical as theoretical since each stud farm and racetrack (if not every individual consulted) has habits and particularities of its own. For a non-specialist, it presents an incomparable, dreamlike perspective. And that is quite enough to justify its existence.

THE ZERO DEGREE OF COLOUR

Let us polish our shoes, for this always produces something: not only shoes shining like new but, perhaps, as sometimes happens, unusual or even fruitful ideas. I owe to a great shoe-polish brand, now defunct, the idea of an enquiry into the notion of colourlessness and its history in Europe from classical Antiquity down to the present day.

What is colourlessness? How is such a notion to be defined? Twenty-five years ago, a modest tin of polish suggested to me a pre-liminary reply to these questions. Colourlessness is the polychrome; or, at least, colourlessness and the polychrome can be equivalent. Like all brands of polish, this one tried to indicate on the lid of its tin the colour of the product inside it: a black disk for black polish, a navy-blue one for navy-blue polish, a reddish-brown one for wine-coloured polish, a white one for white polish. But what about colourless polish? What was to be done? What colour-disk should be used? The makers had found an unusual solution: they displayed a rainbow on the tin, thereby establishing a strange and provocative synonymy between *colourless* and *polychrome*. Just as a rainbow suggests the complete spectrum of col-ours, similarly a colourless polish was suited to all shoes and all colours of leather. This seems like a paradox: could no colour and too many colours basically come to the same?

Having decided to get to the bottom of this contradiction, I ventured into a long-drawn-out enquiry into the notion of colourlessness, an enquiry that still preoccupies me today, so complex and multiform does it turn out to be. Let me now summarize a few aspects of it, starting with those that can be deduced from lexical data. All modern European languages possess a word in current use that conveys the notion of the colourless: for example, *incolore* in French, *farblos* in German, *colourless* in English, *incoloro* or *incolore* in Italian, *incoloro* in Spanish. All are adjectives that can be turned into nouns. However, defining the notion is no easy matter. Most of the explanations or interpretations suggested by various dictionaries are hesitant, imprecise or even contradictory. Furthermore, they fail to provide a satisfactory synonym; it is as if the notion of colourlessness in itself possessed an element that repelled analysis and precision, if not expression. For instance, here is what is suggested by the *Trésor de la langue française*, the richest and most scholarly work devoted to the French lexicon of the nineteenth and twentieth centuries:

> 'colourless' 1. (in the literal sense): that which has no clearly determined colour, no colour of its own and no shade (*syn.* limpid, transparent, pale); 2. (in a figurative sense): that which lacks clarity or brilliance, is expressionless, lacking in originality and personality (*syn.* dull, monotonous, lacklustre).

Ordinary dictionaries for the general public are neither more precise nor more explicit and are content to approach the meanings of the word by suggesting the same synonyms or others that are equally approximate, if not more so: 'discoloured', 'boring', 'insipid', 'uniform'. Strangely enough, very few works dare to define the word 'colourless' with the simple words 'without colour'. On the other hand, a number of them suggest, as synonyms, the terms 'white' and 'grey'. Where language is concerned, colourlessness is always coloured.

Likewise for images. The difficulties encountered by vocabulary when it comes to expressing this notion recur on an even larger scale in images and works of art. How can drawing, painting and engraving convey this idea of colourlessness? How can one indicate or suggest an absence of colour by means of colours? That is not just a theoretical question. In attempts to resolve it, Western artists, down through the centuries, have devised a variety of solutions. None of them has been universally accepted but they all constitute historical documentation regarding the manner in which every period, every society and every kind of technique have tackled the problems of colour.

In ancient societies, colourlessness is often presented as an absence of colouring material, sometimes as the colour of the item that bears the image, whatever that may be; more rarely it is assimilated to transparency, shadow, an absence of light. Since the introduction of printing and engraving, it is mainly represented as white, the colour of background paper which, in the West, plays the role of colourlessness. But black and grey gradually came to join white in this role. So, nowadays, Western culture has at its disposal three vectors for conveying what is at stake and the different nuances of all that which, for one reason or another, is thought of, classified or represented as being colourless: grey, white and black-and-white. The latter is binary and, ever since Newton and his discovery of the spectrum, it constitutes a world that stands in contrast to that of colours. Many techniques and practices for creating images (photography, cinema, television . . .) continue to set in opposition on the one hand colour and, on the other, black-and-white. But the opposition is not as strong as it was fifty or a hundred years ago. The not-so-distant day will come when, not only in social codes and matters of sensibility but also in scientific theories and knowledge, that opposition will probably disappear.

White, employed on its own, continues, however, to embody the idea of colourlessness, as if the link between the two notions, which emerged in the fifteenth century with the diffusion of printed books and engraved images, still preserved all its relevance: in many domains involving texts and images, the zero degree of colour is the white of paper. But information technology and digital images are now beginning to change this way of regarding white, so quite soon white will again be regarded as a colour in its own right. Over the past decades, for many artists, creators and even scientific colourists, that is what has happened to black.

As for grey, it embodies not so much colourlessness or something beyond colourlessness, as, above all, that which is neutral – a 'chromatic neutral', if that expression makes any sense at all. On these grounds it seems to draw in its wake all colours that are neither bright nor bold, all those that dare not declare their name and shade forcefully and that fall into the range of half-and-half tones, 'natural' or even pastel hues.

One certainly becomes aware of this in the fashion world when, every year, around the month of April or May, magazines and advertisements resort to slogans such as 'this summer experience (or dare) a return to colours'. As if colours had ever gone away! For creative artists, stylists, architects and decorators, the real colours are the bright ones: red, yellow, blue, green, purple, orange, seldom black or white, let alone grey. Although not colourless, today grey, probably more than white, embodies the zero degree of colour, or rather, given that it is not truly colourless, the lowest degree of colour.

It sometimes shares this position with the monochrome. In several domains – clothing, advertising, the decorative arts – a single colour, whatever it may be, is no longer enough to 'produce colourfulness'. To exist, to be effective, to 'function' fully, colour requires an interplay of associations or oppositions and combinations of a wide range of colours. It would seem that, to a contemporary eye, nothing is colourful unless it involves two or three colours or even many more, even though a great number of colours can sometimes tend toward colourlessness. Too much colour kills colour, as in the image on the tin of polish that prompted me to take off on this theme.

In Western cultures, today as yesterday, extremes attract each other and fuse, and systems reverse and clash, seeming to underline the vanity of any analysis or even any discourse on the subject. It is as if, always and everywhere, colours only speak to other colours.

A PART THAT STANDS FOR THE WHOLE

Toward the end of his life, my father would sometimes leave the retirement home to which he had retreated and come and spend a few days with me, in our house in Normandy. The journey was short and the visit brief, so not much was required in the way of luggage: a single suitcase was enough. My father possessed two suitcases. They were identical, made of a grey canvas and, round the outside, each was equipped with a thin strap as decoration or for added strength. Those straps indicated the difference between them: one was green, the other navy-blue. For my father, the colour of the strap determined the name by which the suitcase was known: the grey suitcase with a green strap became 'the green suitcase'; the one with a blue strap was 'the blue suitcase'. It was a perfect synecdoche in which the part stood for the whole. There was no mention of grey, a colour which, it must be said, my father, unlike me, did not like.

At first this way of naming the suitcases shocked me, and this led us into specious arguments about figures of speech and the differences between the real colour and the colour named. My father quite rightly pointed out to me that taking a part for a whole or a whole for a part was a common feature of language and constituted a particular case of metonymy. He reminded me that the press daily adopted such figures of speech: 'London has recalled its ambassador', 'France won a medal in the 1,500 metres', 'Thirty sails set out in the regatta', 'The train belched out horrible smoke' . . . He was quite right. Yet I continued to split hairs and unfairly objected that such a use of language could not be applied to colours, a domain that I reckoned to be altogether unique – or to suitcases, objects that I considered to be ridiculous.

A few years later, an item of documentation on the sixteenth century showed me how wrong I was and that such a way of expressing oneself was by no means new. The document listed items that made up the wardrobe of a princess of the house of d'Este. She was Eléonore, the niece of the duke Hercules I, who died in Ferrara in 1527. The inventory, drawn up at her death by two notaries, itemized the clothes of the princess and classified her dresses in terms of colours: six red dresses, four blue dresses, three green dresses, and so on. Now, thanks to other documents – chronicles, portraits, bills and letters – we know that the young woman always wore white. She is indeed certainly dressed in white in two portraits, one of which is a splendid painting by an unknown artist, preserved in the museum of the Jagellon University in Cracow. Were the notaries mistaken? Does this mean that a historian of the sixteenth century can no longer place his trust in inventories drawn up after death – documents that he has for years believed to be more trustworthy than any others? No, the notaries were not mistaken and their inventory remains credible. But they had taken a part for the whole and named the princess's dresses not after their dominant colour, but after the colour of their belts, ribbons and other accessories. In the case of Eléonore d'Este, one should understand that a 'red dress' is a white dress with a red belt; a 'blue dress' is a white dress with blue ribbons, and so on.

In the course of my researches, I have noticed that such turns of phrase are common in ancient documentation, possibly more so than they are today. They prompt a historian to reflect upon the credibility of documentation, whether it be in a written text or an illustration. For neither reproduces the coloured reality as a colour photograph would. If a medieval chronicler tells us that a certain king entered a certain town on a certain day, clad in a blue cloak, that does not mean to say either that he was really wearing blue on that day or that he was not. But that is not the way that problems are presented either in texts or in images.

Such inconsistencies often stem from a synecdoche, a figure of speech which, as we have seen above, takes a part for the whole. One frequently comes across them in Latin epic (Virgil both uses them and misuses them) and they continued to appear down the centuries. Even today, in a house where all the rooms have blue curtains, we will refer to 'the yellow room' when we mean the room which, although decorated in blue material, is distinct from the other rooms in that the hangings are trimmed along the top by a thin yellow braid. One would be mistaken if one thought that the expression 'the yellow room' meant a room truly entirely yellow. Daily life, correspondence, professional activities, the law, literature and advertisements all produce numerous documents in which a part stands for the whole and in which the colour named does not correspond to the dominant colour.

Historians, journalists, sociologists and researchers of every kind should therefore be prudent and not take chromatic information literally for often it aims not to describe reality in the first degree but to express it otherwise, in a partial, indirect or graphic way.

THE GREEK BLUE

We sometimes find it hard to recognize that our ancestors had definitions, classifications and even perceptions of colour different from our own. I have often noticed this in lectures on the history of colours. Our present knowledge is received as the truth and our sensibilities are regarded as norms. However much historians constantly remind us that the past should not be judged by the yardstick of the present and that what we know now is not the truth but simply a stage in the history of knowledge, it does no good. The scholars of today are considered to know more than those of the past and our values are regarded as absolute. Today, it is no easy matter to explain what cultural relativism in space is; it is even harder to explain what relativism in time is.

Actually, this inability to see that everything in these domains is cultural is not limited to our own period. At the time when positivism was triumphant, toward the end of the nineteenth century and at the beginning of the twentieth, where colours were concerned, great historians, famous philologists and prestigious neurologists proposed a reductive scientism which, one century later, we find astonishing. The file on the blue of ancient Greece provides a good example. Furthermore, it has strong historiographic implications.

On the basis of the rarity of blue tones in their material culture and their daily lives and of the hesitations of the Greek lexicon regarding the name of this colour, a number of historians and philologists have wondered whether the Greeks were blind to blue. In Greek (as in Latin, but to a lesser degree), blue seems a difficult colour to name on account of the lack of any or several basic, solid and recurrent terms such as exist for white, for red and for black. The two most frequently used words are *glaukos* and *kyaneos*. Originally, the latter was probably a term that designated some mineral or metal. Its root is not Greek and for a long time its meaning remained imprecise. In the Homeric period, it qualified both the light blue of eyes and the black of some mourning garment, but never the blue of the sky or the sea. It has also been pointed out that, in Homer, out of sixty adjectives used to qualify the elements or the landscape in the *Iliad* and the *Odyssey*, only three were true colour adjectives; on the other hand, terms relating to light are very numerous. In the classical period, *kyaneos* designated a generally dark colour: dark blue, to be sure, but also purple, black and brown. In fact, it expressed the feeling of the colour rather than any colouration. As for *glaukos*, which existed already in the archaic period and which Homer frequently uses, it means sometimes green, sometimes grey, sometimes blue, occasionally even yellow or brown. But what it really conveys is an idea of pallor or a weak concentration of colour rather than a truly well-defined colouration. That is why it can be used just as well for the colour of water as for that of eyes, leaves or honey.

Conversely, to qualify the manifestly blue colour of certain objects, plants or minerals, Greek authors sometimes use colour-terms that do not fall into the range of blues. For flowers, for example, irises, periwinkles and bluebells may be called 'red' (*erythros*), 'green' (*prasos*) or 'black' (*melas*). As for the sea and the sky, they may be any colour or shade, but are never described as blue. Hence the question that was raised in the mid nineteenth century: did the Greeks see blue? And if they did, did they see it as we see it today? To these questions, certain scholars have replied in the negative, advancing evolutionist theories as to the capacities of colour-vision: men and women who belong to technically and intellectually 'evolved' societies – or to ones claimed to be so – such as contemporary Western societies, are more capable of distinguishing and naming a wide range of colours than those who belonged to ancient societies or ones judged to be 'primitive'.

Up until World War I, these theories provoked passionate arguments. Biologists and neurologists flung themselves into the battle, took over the questions that had been debated by historians and philologists and sometimes imposed their views. Those views still have their supporters, although to me they seem indefensible (I am thinking, for example, of the conclusions reached by B. Berlin and P. Kay in their work entitled *Basic Color Terms*, published in 1969). The problem is not only that they are based on an imprecise and dangerous ethnocentric concept (for on the basis of what criteria can anyone decide whether a society is 'evolved' or 'primitive' – who decides?). They also confuse the phenomenon of vision (which is partly biological) with that of perception (which is largely cultural). Moreover, they forget or ignore the sometimes considerable difference that exists, in every period, in every society and for every individual, between the real colour, the colour perceived and the colour named. The absence or imprecision of blue in the Greek colour lexicon should first be studied in relation to that lexicon, its formation and its functioning, and next in relation to the value-systems that underlie it and the societies that use it; but never in relation to people's neurobiological apparatus. Cones and rods are one thing, colour-terms quite another.

The vision apparatus of the ancient Greeks was identical to that of people of the twenty-first century. But problems of colour cannot be reduced to biological and neurobiological questions. If the ancient Greeks seldom name blue, that is probably because, in their daily life as in their symbolic world, blue was a colour that played practically no role, or at least played a far weaker one than white, red, black or yellow. These problems are not physiological or neurobiological; they are lexical, ideological and symbolic. Humans do not live alone; they live in a society.

THE DEMISE OF NUANCES

I studied some of the questions mentioned above in a work published by the Éditions du Seuil in 2000, entitled *Bleu. Histoire d'une couleur* (Blue. The History of a Colour). It represented the findings of about twenty years of research and several years of lecturing on the social history of colours in Europe. Blue was obviously not the sole subject of my study but it did constitute the guiding thread through a long-term history of colours from the Neolithic down to the end of the twentieth century. The book was well received and was translated into fifteen or so languages. However, to my great surprise, the few criticisms that it provoked did not relate to the chapters with which I was the least satisfied and which, I knew, were written too hastily and sometimes based on second-hand documentation (the eighteenth and nineteenth centuries, on which I am no specialist) – but instead concerned the Roman period, where I felt on firmer ground and in which my research on Latin texts was all first-hand.

I had written that blue played no more than a discreet role in ancient Rome in not only social life and material culture but also religious practices and the world of symbols. I had added that the Romans were not fond of blue (for them, it was the colour of barbarians, Germans or Celts) and that, in Rome, in the Imperial period, having blue eyes made one feel inferior. In women, they indicated loose living; in men, they were considered ridiculous. Finally, I had emphasized that, generally speaking, it was not easy to name the colour blue in classical Latin. To be sure, terms did exist for the colour, but they were unstable and imprecise, even polysemic, starting with the most frequently used of them: *caeruleus*. In fact, that is why all the Romance languages stemming from Latin, when they constructed their colour vocabulary, chose for blue two words borrowed from other languages: *bleu* (blue) comes from the Germanic languages, and *azur* comes from Arabic. On all these points I thought that I had been clear and that I had provided evidence for my allegations. I had never written that blue was absent from Roman life nor that in Rome nobody had blue eyes, let alone that the Latin lexicon possessed no term to name this colour.

Yet that was the understanding of various readers, some journalists ('Pastoureau denies the existence of blue in ancient Rome') and even a few colleagues. They all presented me triumphantly with evidence of my 'errors' – extracts from texts, archeological evidence (glass objects, mosaics and so on) – showing, by these very tokens, that for them *absence* and *rarity* meant the same thing and that a qualified opinion, prudently expressed, using adverbs of time, frequency and quantity, were no longer intelligible or acceptable in this day and age.

The example of the Roman blue is in itself anecdotal, but it reflects disturbing modes of sensibility and comprehension. A few years ago I gave a course of lectures in Geneva on the history of pigments in European painting, in which I explained to my students that, between the mid sixteenth century and the early nineteenth, the colour yellow was used sparingly and was less present in painting than red, blue, brown and black. A few weeks later, in several of their essays, I found that those same students had written that in Europe, between the sixteenth and the nineteenth centuries, yellow was absent from paintings! Conversely, when, on another occasion, I delivered a talk on a similar subject to a non-university audience and again underlined this rarity of yellow in the painters of the sixteenth and seventeenth centuries, I found myself, at the end of the lecture, rejecting several counter-examples that were supposed to prove that I had been talking arrant nonsense. Here too, it proved impossible to express oneself in a nuanced manner, to present facts in a relative fashion or to reposition them in their precise context. It was as if, to be understood, every statement had to be general, absolute and clear-cut and every answer to a question had to fit into a set of multiple-choice questions or be 'processed' (another horrible term) on line.

When speaking of language, there is now practically no room for variables, subtleties, restrictions, exceptions or hesitations. Doubt is no longer a tool for thinking, intuition is no longer an instrument of research (indeed, how could one set about introducing intuition into the sacrosanct computer?). Cultural relativism has become scientifically incorrect and politically suspect. It has to be either *yes* or *no*, never *perhaps*; it is *black* or it is *white*, never *grey*, let alone pearl-grey or turtle-dove grey. Linking words, nuancing adverbs and concessive subordinate propositions are now grammatical elements that are obscure and useless. Words such as *possibly* [*éventuellement*] and *probably* are considered synonyms, and the subtleties that accompany them are today undetectable to many of our contemporaries. On the other hand, the use of adverbs such as *absolutely* or *totally* has become all-pervasive, as have all superlative forms. In Western languages, the word *very* is nowadays one of the most used and the most abused. There is no room any more for nuances, the relative or ambivalence.

In such a situation, how does one pursue the profession of a historian? How can one be a researcher in the humanities? How can one speak of colours and all their aspects? How can one speak of art or poetry? How can we express our feelings, our anxieties and our hesitations? How can we speak of our memories and our dreams?

SPEAKING OF COLOURS WITHOUT SHOWING THEM

The present book contains no pictures. Not without reason. I realized quite early on that it is perfectly possible to speak of colours without showing them. First at the university, where the inevitable breakdown of the slide-projector – probably the most recalcitrant object ever invented by human beings – has often obliged me to improvise and speak about the role of colours in this or that domain of medieval art, without being able to show a single image. Then on the radio, where it is clearly impossible to project any slides but where I perceived that devoting an hour or even longer to colours did not upset listeners in any way. And finally in my books, where figures and plates are not always necessary. The present work provides an example: is the reader bothered by the absence of coloured images? I do not think so. On the contrary, I believe that colours are first and foremost concepts, ideas, intellectual categories. Next they become words, that is to say capricious labels that may vary in time and in space and that often set reality at a distance. If we wish to speak of colours, we are the prisoners of those words. Lastly, but only lastly, colours are matter, light, perceptions, sensations.

This order of priorities in the definitions of colour explains why the theories and classifications of scientists impact so little upon the ideological and symbolic practices of colour. It is an order that also helps to explain to a historian why, in a given society, changes are so rare and so slow. Colours are abstractions; they do not need to be materialized in order to exist. Indeed, rendering them material often has the effect of making them lose some of their affective and significant force. On account of this, technical mutations, new materials, new lights and even social transformations influence their evolution very little. There is no denying that such an evolution does take place, but it is slow; and new factors never totally eliminate those that preceded them.

Besides, colours concern everyone, really everyone. Each one of us has some idea of colour: so there is no need to show something red, green or yellow in order to speak effectively about it. On the contrary, showing the colour sometimes spoils one's discourse, diverting it to the problem of nuances and fixing the onlooker's mind upon one particular tinge, a particular material aspect that will prevent him from allowing his mind to wander freely in the infinite fields of meaning and dreaming. Sometimes, to show a colour is to impoverish it. Besides, this often has the effect of submitting one to the caprices and treachery of reproductions, whatever their nature and their quality. Of course, in some fields it is indispensable to show the colour – artistic creation, for example – but there are others in which one can do without them – in fact, it is better to do without them, as I have learnt from my teaching experience. It is not possible to speak about the works of this or that painter without displaying them, so one has to project images, even though these are more or less always misleading. On the other hand, the history of dyes and dyeing can be taught without showing a single image, if one starts off by examining the relevant texts – those concerning rules, techniques, professional matters and book-keeping. Dyers often have more to teach us about the history of colours than painters do. The history of painting is one (fascinating) thing, but the history of colours is another that is far vaster.

Let us return to the power of words and consider the example of the mail-order catalogues that have been studied by my friend Philippe Fagot. Up until the 1930s, colour was absent from these catalogues and all their images were drawings, nearly always printed in black and white. Certain luxury catalogues were accompanied by samples, but these were rare. Usually colours and their different shades were simply named, not shown. This seems not to have bothered several generations of customers, who were content to make do with descriptions and ordinary words such as *blue, red, green, brown, grey* and *black*. Sometimes a particular shade was given: *navy-blue, light grey, pale yellow, dark red*. The lexicon remained simple and accessible. Later, before and after World War II, colour made an appearance – not yet in the form of colour photographs, but in that of modest, framed colour charts. As a child, I was attracted by these colour charts. I would cut them out, collect them and stick them into an exercise-book (now lost, unfortunately). The shades that were reproduced were not exactly those of the fabrics or garments for sale, but attempts were made to make them as close as possible. The rubrics did likewise and enumerated not just the major categories of colours but also the nuances that were available: *gooseberry, peony, apricot, mimosa, almond, fawn, nut-brown*. This vocabulary was intended to be more precise than that of the past, but it was, in fact, less intelligible. Some formulations, in truth, had no link with reality: 'This article is available in *fashionable red, fragrant green, Pondicherry blue.*' Even for contemporaries, such expressions in no way indicated the shades of these reds, greens and blues. Later on, in the late fifties, colour photography made its appearance in catalogues and was soon used everywhere. As it did so, it liberated the colour lexicon: expressions and formulations for the colours illustrated, with no relation at all to the actual tones on offer, multiplied.

In this domain, the most spectacular case was probably that of stockings and tights. For a long time, as for everything to do with feminine lingerie, the vocabulary had been limited to simple, modest words: *grey, brown, white, black, beige*, made more precise by adjectives as common as *light, dark* or *medium*. Then, between 1920 and 1930, as the colour ranges became more subtle, the publicity more raucous, the competition keener, more ambitious terms appeared, borrowed from animals, vegetables and minerals: *ivory, chamois, mole, mouse, turtle-dove, chestnut, clay, slate, anthracite*. The sense remained clear even if the exact shade was imprecise. The next stage accentuated that imprecision and introduced into this specialized lexicon words that were more vague but more enticing. They corresponded to colourations that were hard to name but that the colour-charts and, already, the photographs showed, and were there above all for their evocative power: *dawn, patina, smoke, amber, cloud, mist, dust*. However, it was the next stage, already well established in the 1960s, that truly marked a disconnection that has ever since become increasingly noticeable. Now the terms chosen no longer relate to any colouration, however imprecise, but to an impression, an atmosphere, a desire, a dream: *intoxication, evanescence, disenchantment, not this evening, as usual* and the following sublime *in-between perhaps and not quite*, used to qualify an ineffable shade of grey.

'In-between perhaps and not quite': is this not the very colour of life?

What is colour?

It is impossible to define a colour univocally, as I emphasized right at the start of this book and as I wish to insist now, at the end of it. For the humanities, everything is cultural, strictly cultural. So let us now, for the last time, indulge in a little history and, in conclusion, recall how, in the course of the centuries, colour has been defined first as matter, then as light, and ultimately as sensation. Our present knowledge and behaviour patterns are, to some extent, the legacy of that triple definition.

In a number of language families, the typology of the word that designates colour testifies to the way in which colour was initially conceived and perceived as matter, an envelope that covers beings and things. This is particularly true of the Indo-European languages. The Latin word *color*, for example, from which the Italian, French, Spanish, Portugese and English words for colour all derived, is connected with the large family of the verb *celare*, meaning 'to hide', 'to envelop', 'to conceal': colour is what conceals, covers up, clothes. It is a material reality, a film and second skin or surface that conceals bodies. The same idea is to be found in Greek: the word *khroma* (colour), is derived from the word *khrōs* (skin, the body's surface). The same goes for Germanic languages: the German term *Farbe*, to give but one example, comes from **farwa*, the common Germanic word that meant 'form', 'skin', 'envelope'. Other languages, in no sense European, convey a similar idea: colour seems originally to have been a material, an envelope, a film.

However, a lexicon is one thing, the theories of scholars and philosophers quite another. At an early date, in Europe, colour ceased to be regarded solely as matter and became, in addition and above all, light; or rather, a fraction of light. Aristotle was one of the first to see colour as a weakening of white light and it was he who proposed the most ancient chromatic scale known, ranging from the lightest to the darkest: white, yellow, red, green, black. We should note that on this Aristotelian scale, blue is absent. Not until the Middle Ages did it come to take its place in between green and black.

This scale of colours remained the basic scientific order right down to the seventeenth century, to be precise until 1665–6, the years in which Isaac Newton carried out his famous experiments with the prism and succeeded in decomposing the white light of the sun into different coloured rays. In doing so, he set before the scientific world a new order of colours: the spectrum. It is an order in which there is now no place either for black or for white and in which the colours form a sequence that bears no relation to earlier ones: violet, indigo, blue, green, yellow, orange, red. In most domains relating to the scientific world, this spectral classification of colours progressively imposed itself as the basic physico-chemical order. It was even projected upon such a meteorological phenomenon as the rainbow, the representation of which has always remained a matter of trial and error. Whereas ancient societies saw in a rainbow only three or four colours, our eyes today tend to distinguish seven: the colours of the spectrum. Not that we actually see those seven colours. But ever since primary school, we have all been taught that there are seven colours in the rainbow; so that is what we see, or at least what we think we see.

Defining colour as light, not as matter, constituted an important change for the physical sciences and even, from the eighteenth century onward, for a number of crafts; scientists have gradually learnt to measure colours as wave-lengths and artisans have learnt to divide them into multiple shades. The century of the Enlightenment was also that of colour charts. From that time on, colour was measurable, controllable and reproducible and seemed to have lost some of its mystery – so much so that even artists began to submit to scientific theories: they endeavoured to construct their palettes around the spectrum, distinguishing primary and complementary colours and believing – somewhat naively – in the laws of optics and perception. Later, the neurosciences, in their turn, emphasized the importance of perception and proclaimed that colour was not just a material envelope or a physical phenomenon, but also a sensation: the sensation of a coloured effect, received by the eye and transmitted to the brain. This is thought to be due to the conjunction of three elements: a source of light, an object on which this light falls and a receptive organ, a human being equipped with the complex apparatus – both biological and cultural – constituted by the eye–brain pair.

Today, opinions are beginning to diverge as human beings, as receivers, are experimentally replacing themselves by a simple recording apparatus. For the hard sciences, what is recorded is still colour, measured in wave-lengths. For the humanities, what is recorded is not colour but light: colour only exists if it is perceived, that is to say if it is not only seen by the eyes but also, and most importantly, apprehended and decoded by the memory, one's knowledge and one's imagination. This is what Goethe was suggesting when, already in Part III of his *Farbenlehre*, published in 1810, he asked the following question: 'Is a red dress still red when nobody is looking at it?' To this fundamental question he replied in the negative. So do I.

The colours of a physicist or a chemist are thus not those of a neurologist or a biologist. But nor are those of the latter those of a historian, a sociologist or an anthropologist. For them – and in general for all the humanities – colour is defined and studied primarily as a social factor. It is society, more than nature, pigment, the eye or the brain, that 'makes' colour, gives it definition and meaning, establishes its codes and values, organizes how it is used and determines its effects.

For a historian, to speak of colour is firstly to speak of the history of words and linguistic factors, pigments and colouring agents, and painting and dyeing techniques. But it is also, and more than anything, to speak of its place in daily life, of the codes and systems that accompany it, of the regulations produced by the authorities, of the morals and symbols established by religions, and of the speculations of scientists and the inventions of artists. There are thus a great many fields of enquiry and reflection and they pose all kinds of questions for researchers in the humanities. Essentially, colour constitutes a multidisciplinary field of observation. However, certain domains turn out to be more fruitful than others, in particular those of dyes, fabrics and clothing. It is probably there, rather than in painting and artistic creation, that chemical, technical and material problems intermingle most closely with social, ideological and symbolic factors. In any society, fabrics and clothing constitute the foremost substrata of colour, the foremost chromatic codes and the foremost classificatory systems. The prime function of colour is often to classify: to associate, oppose, distinguish and create hierarchies; to classify beings and things, animals and plants, individuals and groups, places and times, ideas and dreams; and memories too . . .

To this end, contrary to what is generally believed, most societies have depended on a restricted palette. For a long time, in numerous cultures, three colours have counted for more than all the rest, at least at ideological and symbolic levels: white, red and black; that is to say, white and its two opposites. Subsequently, as the centuries passed, and in accordance with modalities that varied a great deal from one culture to another, three other colours eventually joined the first three, bringing the number of basic colours to six: white, red, black, green, yellow and blue.

That is what happened in Western societies: the early triad of white-red-black remained predominant from the Neolithic (or even earlier) until the heart of the Middle Ages, when the promotion of the three other colours occurred. This mutation took place between the twelfth and the fourteenth centuries. Since that time, nothing much has changed. Despite the progress made in the sciences and physico-chemical theories, despite the discovery of the spectrum, despite the distinction between primary and complementary colours, and despite a refusal to consider black and white as colours in their own right, the West has continued to live by a six-colour system: white, red, black, green, yellow and blue. These are the colours that children and people questioned in the street cite most often when asked to name colours. Those that come next – orange, pink, purple, brown and grey – are only half-colours or rather 'second-rank' colours. And then what? Then nothing, at least no true colours that can be isolated and classified, only nuances and nuances of nuances.

Such, rapidly summarized, is the way in which colours have evolved in Europe and the West. Elsewhere, the history of colours has in many cases evolved in accordance with different rhythms and other schemas and variables. Certain cultures do not isolate coloured units in the Western manner, but rely on parameters of their own. In black Africa, up until recent times, what mattered was to decide not whether a colour was red, green, yellow or blue, but whether it was dry or wet, smooth or rough, soft or hard, muted or sonorous. Such are the parameters around which colour-vocabulary has been constructed in a number of African languages. For these, colour is not something in itself, let alone a phenomenon that stems solely from sight. It is apprehended in unison with other sensory parameters. The same likewise obtains in other regions of the world, Central Asia for example, or the Great North. There, Western definitions of colour are not recognized.

These differences between societies are fundamental and should constantly be borne in mind even if, as the centuries have passed, the West has tended to impose upon the entire planet a good many of its theories, practices and value-systems. Today, almost everywhere in the world, there are six basic colours, the legacy sometimes of a distant past, sometimes of a more recent one. Those colours are impossible to define, unlike the second-rank colours, for they have no natural referent or object. The terms that designate them are neither concrete nor warranted.

Let us, just once more, allow the last word to the philosopher Ludwig Wittgenstein. He was the author of a sentence that is perhaps the most important ever written on this subject. It seems, better than any other, the right one to round off this book of memories devoted to the unique and elusive object that is colour:

If we are asked, *what do the words red, blue, black, white* mean, we can, of course, immediately point to things which have these colours. But our ability to explain the meaning of these words goes no further. (*Bemerkungen über die Farben*, I, 68; *Remarks on Colour*, I, 68, p. 11c)

Bibliography

General works

Birren, Faber, *Color. A Survey in Words and Pictures*, New York, 1961.

Conklin, Harold C., 'Color Categorization', *The American Anthropologist*, 75/4, 1973, pp. 931–42.

Gage, John, *Color and Culture. Practice and Meaning from Antiquity to Abstraction*, London, 1993.

Gerschel, Lucien, 'Couleurs et teintures chez divers peoples européens', *Annales ESC*, 1966, pp. 608–63.

Indergand, Michel and Fagot, Philippe, *Bibliographie de la couleur*, Paris, 1984–8, 2 vols.

Junod, Philippe and Pastoureau, Michel, eds., *Regards croisés sur la couleur du Moyen Age au XXe siècle*, Paris, 1994.

Meyerson, Ignace, ed., *Problèmes de la couleur*, Paris, 1957.

Pastoureau, Michel, *Bleu. Histoire d'une couleur*, Paris, 2000.

Pastoureau, Michel, *Noir. Histoire d'une couleur*. Paris, 2009.

Pastoureau, Michel and Simmonet, Dominique, *Le Petit Livre des couleurs*, Paris, 2006.

Portmann, Adolf and Ritsema, Rudolf, eds., *The Realms of Colour. Die Welt der Farben*, Leiden, 1974 (*Eranos Yearbook*, 1972).

Pouchelle, Marie-Christine, ed., *Paradoxes de la couleur*, Paris, 1990 (special number of the review *Ethnologie française*, 20/4, Oct.–Dec. 1990).

Tornay, Serge, ed., *Voir et nommer les couleurs*, Nanterre, 1978.

Vogt, Hans Heinrich, *Farben und ihre Geschichte*, Stuttgart, 1973.

Zahan, Dominique, 'L'homme et la couleur', in Jean Poirier, ed., *Histoire des moeurs*, vol. I, *Les Coordonnés de l'homme et la Culture matérielle*, Paris, 1990, pp. 115–80.

Lexicons and language

André, Jacques, *Étude sur les termes de couleurs dans la langue latine*, Paris, 1949.

Baum, Maggy and Boyeldieu-Duyck, Chantal, *Passepoil, piqûres, paillettes. Dictionnaire de fil, d'aiguilles et d'étoffes*, preface by Lydia Flem, Paris, 2008.

Berlin, Brent and Kay, Paul, *Basic Color Terms. Their Universality and Evolution*, Berkeley, 1969.

Crosland, Maurice P., *Historical Studies in the Language of Chemistry*, London, 1962.

Favre, Jean-Paul and November, André, *Color and Communication*, Zurich, 1979.

Grossmann, Maria, *Colori e lessico: studi sulla struttura semantica degli aggetivi di colore in catalano, castigliano, italiano, romano, latino ed ungherese*, Tübingen, 1988.

Indergand, Michel, Lanthony, Philippe and Sève, Robert, *Dictionnaire des termes de la couleur*, Avallon, 2007.

Jacobson-Widding, Anit, *Red-White-Black, as a Mode of Thought*, Stockholm, 1979.

Kristol, Andres M., *Color. Les langues romanes devant le phenomène couleur*, Berne, 1978.

Magnus, Hugo, *Histoire de l'évolution du sens des couleurs*, Paris, 1878.

Meunier, Annie, 'Quelques remarques sur les adjectifs de couleur', *Annales de l'Université de Toulouse*, 11/5, 1975, pp. 37–62.

Mollard-Desfour, Annie, *Dictionnaire des mots et expressions de la couleur*: *Le Bleu*, Paris, 1998; *Le Rouge*, Paris, 2000; *Le Rose*, Paris, 2002; *Le Noir*, Paris, 2005; *Le Blanc*, Paris, 2007.

Wierzbicka, Anna, 'The Meaning of Color Terms: Chromatology and Culture', *Cognitive Linguistics*, 1/1, 1990, pp. 99–150.

Dyes and pigments

Bomford, David et al., *Art in the Making: Impressionism*, London, 1990.

Brunello, Franco, *L'arte della tintura nella storia dell'umanita*, Vicenza, 1968.

Cardon, Dominique and Du Châtenet, Gaëtan, *Guide des teintures naturelles*, Neuchâtel and Paris, 1990.

Delamare, François and Guineau, Bernard, *Les Matériaux de la couleur*, Paris, 1999.

Feller, Robert L. and Roy, Ashok, *Artists' Pigments. A Handbook of their History and Characteristics*, Washington, 1985–6, 2 vols.

Guineau, Bernard, ed., *Pigments et colorants de l'Antiquité et du Moyen Age*, Paris, 1990.

Harley, Rosamond D., *Artists' Pigments (c. 1600–1835)*, 2nd edn, London, 1982.

Hours, Madeleine, *Les Secrets des chefs-d'oeuvre*, Paris, 1988.

Jaoul, Martine, ed., *Des teintes et des couleurs*, exhibition catalogue, Paris, 1988.

Kittel, Hans, ed., *Pigmente*, Stuttgart, 1960.

Montagna, Giovanni, *I pigmenti. Prontuario per l'arte e il restauro*, Florence, 1993.

Pastoureau, Michel, *Jésus chez le teinturier. Couleurs et teintures dans l'Occident medieval*, Paris, 1998.

Reclams Handbuch der künstlerischen Techniken, vol. I, *Farbmittel, Buchmalerei, Tafel- und Leinwandmalerei*, Stuttgart, 1988.

Techné. La science au service de l'art et des civilisations, vol. IV, *La couleur et ses pigments*, 1996.

Varichon, Anne, *Couleurs, pigments et teintures dans les mains des peuples*, Paris, 2000.

Colours, clothing and society

Augé, Marc, *Un ethnologue dans le métro*, Paris, 1986.

Augé, Marc, *Le Métro revisité*, Paris, 2008 (available in English as *In the Metro*, tr. Tom Conley, Minneapolis, 2002).

Batchelor, David, *La Peur de la couleur*, Paris, 2001.

Birren, Faber, *Selling Color to People*, New York, 1956.

Boehn, Max von, *Die Mode. Menschen und Moden vom Untergang der alten Welt bis zum Beginn des zwanzigsten Jahrhunderts*, Munich 1907–25, 8 vols.

Boucher, François, *Histoire du costume en Occident de l'Antiquité à nos jours*, Paris, 1965.

Couleurs, travail et société du Moyen Age à nos jours, exhibition catalogue, Lille, 2004.

Eco, Renate, ed., *Colore: divietti, decreti, discute*, Milan, 1985 (special number of the review *Rassegna*, 23, Sept. 1985).

Fagot, Philippe, 'Rêver la couleur sans la toucher. Mise en scène de la chromaticité par les catalogues de vente par correspondance', in *Couleurs, travail et société du Moyen Age à nos jours*, exhibition catalogue, Lille, 2004, pp. 74–81.

Friedmann, Daniel, *Une histoire du blue-jean*, Paris, 1987.

Harvey, John, *Men in Black*, London, 1995.

Heller, Eva, *Wie Farben wirken, Farbpsychologie, Farbsymbolik, Kreative Farbgestaltung*, 2nd edn, Berlin, 1999 (French translation: *Psychologie de la couleur. Effets et symboliques*, Paris, 2009).

Laufer, Otto, *Farbensymbolik im deutschen Volsbraugh*, Hamburg, 1948.

Lenclos, Jean-Philippe and Lenclos, Dominique, *Les Couleurs de la France. Maisons et paysages*, Paris, 1982.

Lenclos, Jean-Philippe and Lenclos, Dominique, *Les Couleurs de l'Europe. Géographie de la couleur*, Paris, 1995.

Lurie, Alison, *The Language of Clothes*, London, 1982.

Nathan, Harriet, *Levi Strauss and Company, Taylors to the World*, Berkeley, 1976.

Nixdorff, Heide and Müller, Heidi, eds., *Weisse Vesten, roten Roben. Von den Farbordnungen des Mittelalters zum individuellen Farbgeschmak*, exhibition catalogue, Berlin, 1983.

Noblet, Jocelyn de, ed. *Design, miroir du siècle*, Paris, 1993.

Noël, Benoît, *L'Histoire du cinéma couleur*, Croissy-sur-Seine, 1995.

Pastoureau, Michel, *Dictionnaire des couleurs de notre temps. Symbolique et société*, 4th edn, Paris, 2007.

Pastoureau, Michel, 'Du vague des drapeaux', *Le Genre humain*, 20 (*Face au drapeau*), 1989, pp. 119–34.

Rabbow, Arnold, *Lexikon politischer Symbole*, Munich, 1970.

Philosophy and History of Science

Blay, Michel, *Le Conceptualisation newtonienne des phénomènes de la couleur*, Paris, 1983.

Blay, Michel, *Les Figures de l'arc-en-ciel*, Paris, 1995.

Boyer, Carl B., *The Rainbow from Myth to Mathematics*, New York, 1959.

Goethe, Wolfgang, *Zur Farbenlehre*, Tübingen, 1808–10, 2 vols.

Goethe, Wolfgang, *Materialen zur Geschichte der Farbenlehre*, new edn, Munich, 1971, 2 vols.

Halbertsma, K. J. A., *A History of the Theory of Colour*, Amsterdam, 1949.

Lanthony, Philippe, *Des yeux pour peindre*, Paris, 2006.

Lindberg, David C., *Theories of Vision from Al-Kindi to Kepler*, Chicago, 1976.

Newton, Isaac, *Optiks or a Treatise on the Reflexions, Refractions, Inflexions and Colours of Light*, London, 1704.

Pastore, Nicholas, *Selective History of Theories of Visual Perception, 1650–1950*, Oxford, 1971.

Sepper, Dennis L., *Goethe contra Newton. Polemics and the Project of a New Science of Color*, Cambridge, Mass., 1988.

Sève, Robert, *Physique de la couleur. De l'apparence colorée à la technique colorimétrique*, Paris, 1996.

Sherman, Paul D., *Colour Vision in the Nineteenth Century: the Young–Helmholtz–Maxwell Theory*, Cambridge, 1981.

Westphal, John, *Colour: A Philosophical Introduction*, 2nd edn, London, 1991.

Wittgenstein, Ludwig, *Bemerkungen über die Farben*, Frankfurt-am-Main, 1979.

Zuppiroli, Libero et al., *Traité des couleurs*, Lausanne, 2001.

History and Theories of Art

Albers, Josef, *L'Interaction des couleurs*, new edn, Paris, 2008.

Aumont, Jacques, *Introduction à la couleur: des discours aux images*, Paris, 1994.

Brusatin, Manlio, *Storia dei colori*, 2nd edn, Turin, 1983 (French translation: *Histoire des couleurs*, Paris, 1986).

Dittmann, Lorenz, *Farbgestaltung und Farbtheorie in der abendländischen Malerei*, Stuttgart, 1987.

Hall, Marcia B, *Color and Meaning. Practice and Theory in Renaissance Painting*, Cambridge, Mass., 1992.

Imdahl, Max, *Farbe. Kunsttheorische Reflexionen in Frankreich*, Munich, 1987.

Itten, Johannes, *Kunst der Farbe*, 4th edn, Ravensburg, 1961.

Kandinsky, Wassily, *Ueber das Geistige in der Kunst*, Munich, 1912 (English translation: *Concerning the Spiritual in Art*, New York, 1977).

Le Rider, Jacques, *Les Couleurs et les mots*, Paris, 1997.

Lichtenstein, Jacqueline, *La Couleur éloquente. Rhétorique et peinture à l'âge classique*, Paris, 1989.

Roque, Georges, *Art et science de la couleur. Chevreul et les peintres de Delacroix à l'abstraction*, 2nd edn, Paris, 2009.

Rubens contre Poussin. La querelle du coloris dans la peinture française à la fin du XVIIe siècle, exhibition catalogue, Arras, 2004.

Teyssèdre, Bernard, *Roger de Piles et les Débats sur le coloris au siècle de Louis XVI*, Paris, 1957.

A few helpful chronological details

17 June 1947. Born in Paris.

1947–56. Childhood in Montmartre, right at the top of the Butte, where my mother's pharmacy was located.

July 1948. Gino Bartali wins the Tour de France for the second time.

1950–2010. Summer holidays spent in Le Val-André (Côtes-d'Armor).

Spring 1951. The Pastoureau–Carrouges affair: the definitive break in relations between my father and André Breton.

1952–6. I often played in the studio of the painter Marcel Jean, at the foot of the Butte.

1954. My first visits to the Louvre. My earliest experiences as a Wolf-Cub.

Summer 1955. On five consecutive days, I watched *Ivanhoe*, the film directed by Richard Thorpe. I conceived a passion for the Middle Ages.

1957–97. Holidays in and frequent visits to the small Normandy village of Saint-Céneri-le-Gerei (Orne).

1 October 1957. I began my studies at the Lycée Michelet, in Vanves.

1958–60. My first 'chromatic whims': the yellow bike affair and the navy-blue blazer affair.

1960–5. My adolescent passions: colours, heraldry, chess, sports, especially athletics.

Spring 1960. My first encounter with heraldry; in my *lycée*, a teacher of drawing had us copy a sixteenth-century stained-glass coat of arms.

1965–8. Preparatory classes at the Lycée Henri-IV.

1968. Studies at the École nationale des chartes. My thesis on a medieval heraldic bestiary. My earliest serious research on the history of colours.

1972–82. Curator at the department of medals and antiques in the Bibliothèque nationale: a very colourless numismatic world.

1974–5. Military service. Five weeks of classes in Provence; my first and only contact with the tricolour flag. Then eleven months at the Invalides Musée de l'Armée, as the 'scholar' from my military contingent. Here I wrote my first book, *La Vie quotidienne au temps des chevaliers de la Table Ronde* (Daily Life at the Time of the Knights of the Round Table), in the museum's library, which I manned every afternoon, even though no-one ever visited it.

1977. Publication of my first article on the history of colours in the Middle Ages.

1979. *Traité héraldique* (Treatise on heraldry) (Picard).

December 1980. My first visit to the United States (very disappointing).

1982. Appointed *directeur d'études* at the École pratique des hautes etudes. In the course of my twenty-eight years of teaching there, half of my seminars have been devoted to the history and symbolism of colours; the other half to the history of animals.

1991. *L'Étoffe du Diable. Une histoire des rayures et des tissus rayés* (The Stuff of the Devil. A History of Stripes and Striped Materials) (Seuil).

1992. *Dictionnaire des couleurs de notre temps. Symbolique et société contemporaines* (A dictionary of colours in our times. Contemporary symbolism and society) (Bonneton).

1996. Visit to the Vermeer exhibition in The Hague.

1998. *Jésus chez le teinturier. Couleurs et teintures dans l'Occident medieval* (Le Léopard d'or).

2000. *Bleu. Histoire d'une couleur* (Seuil).

2009. *Noir. Histoire d'une couleur* (Seuil).

INDEX